OSPREY COMBAT AIRCRAFT • 53

F-15C EAGLE
UNITS IN COMBAT

SERIES EDITOR: TONY HOLMES

OSPREY COMBAT AIRCRAFT • 53

F-15C EAGLE UNITS IN COMBAT

STEVE DAVIES

OSPREY

PUBLISHING

Front cover
The third day of Operation *Desert Storm* (19 January 1991) saw one of the most exciting engagements of the entire war fought out over the skies of Iraq. Capt Cesar 'Rico' Rodriguez and his wingman Capt Craig 'Mole' Underhill of the 58th TFS/33rd TFW were conducting a fighter sweep ahead of a strike force of F-16s and F/A-18s when they were vectored by an AWACS controller towards a single pop-up threat. Within minutes Rodriguez had been locked up on radar by the approaching MiG-29, forcing him to turn away from the enemy jet in order to spoil its targeting solution. Underhill supported his flight lead by firing an AIM-7 Sparrow, which guided squarely into the Iraqi jet.

Turning back towards the burning MiG after the AWACS controller had spotted a second pop-up threat, Rodriguez detected this second contact of the mission:

'We received another call from the western AWACS, at which point we executed an in-place check turn to the north. I looked up and saw a smoke trail – not a missile trail, but engine smoke – and "Mole" and I simultaneously locked him up. We started going through our ID matrix, and the target displayed a friendly electronic return to both of us. I now directed a VID pass, looking out at about four miles and spotting a silhouette that looked a lot like an F-15 or an F/A-18, so I didn't declare it hostile. At about two miles I looked once again, but I was no longer thinking about taking a pre-merge shot. Instead, I planned to merge with the bogey just 50 ft off of its left wing. As I crossed its wing-line, I saw that the jet was in fact a brown/green-camouflaged Iraqi MiG-29.'

In the scrap that ensued, Rodriguez successfully positioned himself behind the 'Fulcrum', chasing the jet down to the desert floor, where the MiG impacted the ground and cartwheeled for several miles. (*Cover artwork by Mark Postlethwaite*)

In memory of Maj Rhory 'Hoser' Draeger

First published in Great Britain in 2004 by Osprey Publishing
1st Floor Elms Court, Chapel Way, Botley, Oxford, OX2 9LP

ISBN 1 84176 730 1

Edited by Tony Holmes
Page design by Tony Truscott
Cover Artwork by Mark Postlethwaite
Aircraft Profiles by Chris Davey
Scale Drawings by Mark Styling
Index by David Worthington
Origination by Grasmere Digital Imaging, Leeds, UK
Printed in China through Bookbuilders

EDITOR'S NOTE
To make this best-selling series as authoritative as possible, the Editor would be interested in hearing from any individual who may have relevant photographs, documentation or first-hand experiences relating to the world's elite pilots, and their aircraft, of the various theatres of war. Any material used will be credited to its original source. Please write to Tony Holmes via e-mail at: tony.holmes@osprey-jets.freeserve.co.uk

ACKNOWLEDGEMENTS
The author would like to thank Cols Jon 'J B' Kelk, Jay 'Op' Denney, Thomas 'Vegas' Dietz, Cesar 'Rico' Rodriguez and Rick 'Kluso' Tollini (Ret), Lt Cols Larry 'Cherry' Pitts, Tony 'Kimo' Schiavi, Mark 'Mac' McKenzie, Chuck 'Sly' Magill, Craig 'Mole' Underhill, Bob 'Giggs' Hehemann, David 'Abby' Sveden, Greg 'Dutch' Masters, Rob 'Cheese' Graeter and Kathleen Hancox, Capts David Small and Josie Stewart, Lt Joseph Campbell, Ilah Glover and Benjamin Frakenfeld, MSgt Renee Nelson, Erin Zagursky, Col Jarmo Lindberg of The Fighter Tactics Academy, Bob Sanchez of TwoBobs Aviation Graphics and Tom Cooper, who provided me with the bulk of the Iraqi Air Force Order of Battle data in this book and much of the information associated with the Royal Saudi Air Force's 1984 kills.

I am indebted to my proof-readers, all of whom are ex- or current-Eagle 'drivers' – Col (Ret) Doug 'Disco' Dildy, who provided an abundance of changes, suggestions and corrections to the main text, Lt Col Phil 'LeBeau' Nicholson, Troy 'Birdman' Fortmann and Tom 'Eeyore' Murphy. Finally, without the 'usual suspects' this book would have been all but impossible to produce – Caroline, Lt Col Gary 'Reverend' Klett and Capt Randall 'Hacker' Haskin.

CONTENTS

THE EAGLE TAKES FLIGHT

The F-15 Eagle is the most successful fighter in history – at 105.5 enemy kills for zero losses, there is no contest. But the F-15 is not simply the world's most successful fighter. It is an icon of American technological prowess and advancement in the 1960s, and a monument to the US Air Force pilots who re-learned lessons the hard way, often paying with their lives, during the aerial engagements of the Vietnam air war.

America's pilots, who entered the fray over North Vietnam both ill-equipped and tactically constrained by the rules of engagement (ROE) pertaining to this conflict, were confronted by Soviet-built MiG-17s and -21s created according to the founding principles of fighter aircraft design – highly agile, equipped with cannon and simple to operate and maintain. With the help of ground radar known as Ground Control Intercept, the pilots flying the MiGs used high-speed, slashing attacks on US fighter-bomber formations, wreaking havoc with their devastating nose-mounted weaponry and air-to-air missiles (see *Osprey Combat Aircraft 25 - MiG-17/19 Units of the Vietnam War* and *Osprey Combat Aircraft 29 - MiG-21 Units of the Vietnam War*).

Years prior, as the aerospace industry in the United States set about designing the next generation of fighters to replace the venerable F-86 Sabre and its cohorts according to USAF wishes, designers crucially miscalculated the evolving nature of air warfare, and mistakenly concluded that future aerial conflict would share few similarities with that fought in the past. The vast majority of US pilots who had seen action in the Korean War had also fought in World War 2, flying fighters against the Germans or Japanese. With memories of dogfighting still fresh in their minds, therefore, these combat veterans used their finely-honed skills to secure a kill ratio for the F-86 of around 10:1 against a much more numerous foe.

In contrast, the USAF's 1963 study of the future of air warfare – Project *Forecast* – hypothesised that conflicts would now require fighters that would fly high and fast, killing the enemy at long range with missiles that were guided to their targets by radar.

The F-86 created the first American jet ace in the form of Lt Col James Jabara, who ended the Korean War with 15 MiG kills – a testimony to his skills as a pilot, and his traditional dogfighting abilities honed in World War 2, as well as the effectiveness of North America's simple Sabre design. (*USAF*)

Consequently, manoeuvrability and close-range offensive weaponry were low priorities when the next generation of fighter aircraft were built. Interceptors like the F-4 Phantom II and century series fighters which preceded it were built with wings designed to allow them to fly fast at high altitudes, but were poorly-suited to tight manoeuvring.

With the introduction of these aircraft to frontline units from the mid 1950s onwards, the USAF reduced the time it spent teaching pilots air combat manoeuvring (ACM), and instead focused on killing the enemy from extended ranges. Rarely would jets close to 'the merge' to dogfight in the 'old-fashioned' way. As if to reinforce this monumental doctrinal change, the US Navy and Air Force each bought the F-4 without a cannon. The snowball of events that would lead to abysmal performances over Vietnam was building in earnest.

The theory behind destroying targets beyond visual range was sound, but the truth is that even today's technology is not good enough to guarantee a kill every time. Advances in solid-state electronics in the 1960s allowed missiles like the AIM-7 Sparrow to engage targets at medium range (15 to 20 miles), but these had to be non-manoeuvring bombers of the kind that the Soviets would launch to drop nuclear weapons. Against manoeuvrable fighters these missiles were almost useless, as soon became apparent when the F-4 debuted in combat over North Vietnam in 1965.

In order to remedy some of these problems, the US Navy established the Topgun Naval Fighter Weapons School in 1969 (see *Osprey Combat Aircraft 26 - US Navy F-4 Phantom II MiG Killer 1965–70*) to take its best pilots and radar intercept officers and teach them specialised ACM tactics. With the course completed, they would return to their squadrons and convey these tactics to other crews. This training immediately proved its worth, as Navy Phantom II crews enjoyed much more success in combat in 1972 than they had done at any stage during the *Rolling Thunder* campaign, which ran from 1965 to 1968. The USAF created a similar Fighter Weapons School, and its crews also benefited as a result. The *overall* US kill ratio at the end of the Vietnam War was a dismal 2.5:1, although the Navy's ratio had gone from 3:1 in 1969 to 12:1 by 1973.

The F-4 Phantom II was a jack of all trades but master of none. It had been designed with one primary goal in mind – to fly very high and very fast, and to intercept Soviet bombers carrying nuclear weapons. It carried long- and short-range air-to-air missiles, but initially lacked a gun with which to kill the enemy up close. (*USAF*)

AIRCRAFT

It was with these hard-learned lessons in mind that the F-15 was conceived. The process started with an Air Force study into the relative capabilities of Soviet and US fighters. Headed by Gen John P McConnell, it concluded that Soviet interceptors posed a greater threat than had originally been gauged. US Defense Secretary Robert McNamara subsequently allocated FY66 $10 million for the Air Force to commission the design of the ultimate US fighter aircraft and McConnell initiated a study for a new machine.

The study placed greater emphasis on manoeuvrability, anticipated a cost of between $1 and $2 million per airframe and a production run of up to 1000 aircraft in total. With ongoing events in the skies over Vietnam at the forefront of their minds, McConnell's staff initially placed a heavy emphasis on air-to-air capability, much to the chagrin of a budget-conscious Congress that wanted equal emphasis on both air-to-air and air-to-ground capabilities. The study was known as Fighter Experimental (FX).

A Request For Proposal (RFP) was sent to 13 companies on 8 December 1965, after which the eight respondents commenced a four-month Concept Formulation Study in order to refine their designs. No fewer than 500 designs were submitted, all of which were rejected in October 1966 because their air-to-ground features would have negatively impacted the jet's air-to-air role. An internal gun was a common feature in each design, demonstrating that lessons were being learned from Vietnam, but the designs were all far too heavy (60,000 lbs), and bore too close a resemblance to the TFX (Tactical Fighter Experimental) programme from a few years before.

In July 1967 the Soviet Union unveiled its newest interceptor, the MiG-25 'Foxbat'. It was a fast and high-flying interceptor designed to counter the still-born XB-70 Valkyrie bomber, and it sent shockwaves throughout NATO when it broke a number of world speed, altitude, and climb records. Stunned by its apparent dominance, western intelligence analysts overestimated its capabilities, thereby increasing the sense of urgency already driving the FX programme.

A second RFP was duly issued to eight contractors on 11 August 1967, and it was at this stage that work conducted by Maj John R Boyd some three years earlier was integrated for the first time into the design process. Boyd was an Air Force test pilot who had controversially devised the 'energy manoeuvrability (EM)' theory. Simply put, the EM graph allowed designers to take an aerodynamic shape and plot what energy state, lift, drag, and other criteria would be placed upon it at a range of altitudes and airspeeds. Armed with this information, the eight contractors could forecast how well their designs would manoeuvre across the entire flight envelope. Boyd's EM theory directly contributed to dramatically reducing the weight of the submitted designs to nearer the 40,000 lbs mark.

The Air Force and Navy both took advantage of the November 1968 change of Administration in the White House to progress beyond the prototype stages of their individual fighters. The Navy had bowed out of the TFX programme because the aircraft was unsuitable for carrier operations, and had instructed Grumman to commence

full-scale development of what eventually became the F-14 Tomcat. The USAF issued its penultimate FX 'wish-list' in early 1968, the aircraft it wanted being a single-seat fighter that was capable of flying a 260-nautical mile mission on internal fuel, possessing excellent all-round pilot visibility, twin engines and a balanced combination of stand-off and close-in target killing potential. The USAF also wanted survivability and good throttle response from an airframe that could outmanoeuvre and out-gun any enemy fighter that survived the initial beyond visual range (BVR) engagement.

A final Contract Definition Phase document called for a range of criteria to be fulfilled by 30 June 1969, these including a thrust-to-weight ratio approaching 1:1 at combat weight, a fatigue life of 4000 flight hours, 360-degree visibility from the single-seat cockpit and a gross weight of 40,000 lbs. On 23 December 1969 the production contract for the USAF's new fighter interceptor was awarded to the McDonnell Douglas Corporation. Its Aircraft Company division was to prepare for an eventual production run of 749 model 199-B airframes – the US Air Force's new fighter. It was to be called the F-15 Eagle.

KEY TECHNOLOGIES AND SYSTEMS

The 199-B design was tested and developed for two years following the roll-out of F-15A-1-MC serial number 71-0280 from McDonnell Douglas' St Louis, Missouri, plant on 26 June 1972. The prototype made its first flight on 27 July 1972, and production examples finally entered service with the 1st Tactical Fighter Wing (TFW) at Langley AFB, Virginia, in January 1976.

The F-15 Eagle has since matured into the world's most successful fighter. Key to this is a superb radar, excellent supporting avionics and a reliable, maintenance-friendly airframe. Additionally, the simple, fixed geometry, cambered wing design is optimised for high-subsonic manoeuvrability, and confers a 21.5-degree per second sustained turn rate and an equally impressive instantaneous turn rate.

The F-15 Eagle boasted many 'firsts', not least of which was a revolutionary concept that complimented the radar and weapons systems – Hands On Throttle And Stick (HOTAS). This was a euphemism for the science of placing switches and buttons within easy reach of the pilot's thumbs and fingers, and was accomplished by strategically locating them on the throttle and control stick grip. Such ingenuity has since enabled F-15 pilots to score kills in scenarios when they might otherwise have been too busy 'heads down', locating a switch, setting up a series of switches or performing some other labour-

Cuddling up behind the boom of a KC-135A refuelling tanker during trials, this prototype F-15A wears high conspicuity orange markings. An old fighter pilot adage pronounces that if a fighter looks good it will fly well, and the Eagle was no exception to that rule. (*Denis Jenkins via Author*)

intensive task. HOTAS reached peak utility following the implementation of the 1983 Multi-Stage Improvement Program (MSIP), which saw a new throttle and (post-1992) an F-15E stick grip with a greater array of buttons integrated into the jet.

HOTAS was complimented by a Heads Up Display (HUD) that employed two combining glasses, onto which a wide range of flight and weapons system information was projected. It too increased the pilot's awareness by allowing him to keep his eyes outside the jet for longer.

McDonnell Douglas refined the Eagle design in the form of the F-15C/D, which boasted an increased combat radius. First flown on 26 February 1979, the C-model also featured a full avionics fit, including a comprehensive tactical electronic warfare system (TEWS), which had been absent from most A-models, as well as an additional radio (UHF) and strengthened airframe components.

Multiple Stage Improvement Program II (MSIP II) was introduced to F-15C/Ds rolling off the production line in February 1983. The entire F-15 inventory was later retrofitted with MSIP, and 84-0001 – the first upgraded MSIP-II F-15C – was flown in June 1985. MSIP II provided a 25 per cent increase in systems reliability, and briefly saw the installation of the Hughes AN/APG-70, followed by the definitive APG-63(V)I – the latter boasted a faster Central Computer with more memory. Other improvements included the fitment of a new Multi-Purpose Colour Display in place of the existing analogue armament panel, wiring and software to integrate the Joint Tactical Information Distribution System (only fitted to a limited number of airframes, and replaced by Fighter Data Link in 2001), new throttles, a Video Tape Recording System for the HUD and radar for post-flight debriefing and kill validation, TEWS improvements, and support for the AIM-120 AMRAAM (Advanced Medium Range Air-to-Air Missile).

Above and top
The F-15's ergonomic cockpit, HOTAS controls, and superb HUD were revolutionary. These images show the Eagle cockpit following the 1983 MSIP II programme, which introduced to the cockpit a new display and enhanced HOTAS controllers.
(*Author/FJPhotography.com*)

APG-63 RADAR

The F-15A's APG-63 radar was built by Hughes following a parallel tender process to the FX programme, and it is the single most important asset on board the aircraft. Hughes was awarded the contract to produce an advanced radar with an all-weather capability against airborne threats (including AIM-7 guidance provisions, 'look-down, shoot-down' capability and cueing optical tracking systems that might be retrofitted on the jet at a later date, as employed by the air-to-ground F-15E) in 1968. It was also required to build into the APG-63 a limited capability against ground threats.

The $82 million contract issued in October 1970 eventually yielded the APG-63(V)0 radar, which could track targets in ground clutter

The APG-63(V)0 radar was soon superseded by the APG-70 (as seen here installed in an F-15E). The APG-70 offered several advantages over the (V)0, but was itself replaced in some airframes by the APG-63(V)1 years later. Units that deployed to Operation *Desert Storm* were initially equipped with a mix of both, although jets with the newest radars were quickly rushed to the Gulf and swapped with their outdated siblings. (*Author/FJPhotography.com*)

using Doppler shift, and employed high and medium Pulse Repetition Frequencies (PRFs) to track objects at different ranges, altitudes, aspects, and closing speeds, according to various pre-programmed modes selected by the pilot. It represented a quantum leap over existing capabilities, and was tailored for ease of use whilst providing maximum situational awareness (SA) for the pilot.

Several different derivatives and iterations of the APG-63(V)0 have been installed in the Eagle, namely the APG-70, APG-63(V)1, and APG-63(V)2. They can all be characterised as utilising Medium, High and Interleaved Pulse Repetition Frequencies (PRFs), Ground Moving Target Rejection algorithms to reject false ground returns, and a core base of main- and sub-operating modes that are selected according to a range of tactical and environmental factors. The main search mode is Interleaved Mode (Range While Search), which provides a good compromise between scan volume, detection range, and data generation in order to allow long-range air-to-air surveillance to take place. The radar is also reasonably jam-resistant.

ENGAGEMENT TECHNIQUES

The APG-63 and APG-70 feature a series of Track While Scan (TWS) modes, but these were relatively new when the F-15C went to war in the Persian Gulf in 1991, and their use was actively discouraged in favour of the 'real-time' Range While Search (RWS). TWS offered more information on each contact, but was discouraged because it could not support the semi-active radar-homing AIM-7 Sparrow air-to-air missile. It also had a reduced azimuth and elevation coverage. Nor could it detect 'pop up' contacts outside of its comparatively limited search volume (which was smaller than the search volume offered by RWS). Staying in RWS required greater operator skill and discipline because less information about each contact was available, but the benefits of keeping the intercept simple made up for it.

Up until the mid-1990s, Long-Range Scan (APG-63) or Interleave (APG-70) was used to find the target, and the radar was switched to Single-Target Track (STT) mode when the contact came within the AIM-7's dynamic launch zone. STT prompted the radar to focus a thin beam of energy on the target of interest, and instructed it to switch to the High PRFs necessary for AIM-7 guidance. It also generated a wealth of information on the target, including altitude, range, closing velocity, heading, aspect angle, and True Air Speed. This technique was used in nearly every F-15 kill prior to 1992.

By comparison, today's F-15 pilots can complete an entire engagement without ever switching from TWS mode, principally because it features 'native' support for simultaneous multi-target engagement with the newer AIM-120 AMRAAM missile. The 1999 F-15 kills discussed in Chapter 4 were scored in this manner, including the first ever double AIM-120 kills from a single engagement.

Finally, there are several references in this text to Auto Acq (Automatic Acquisition) modes that instantly lock up the first target that falls within a prescribed radar scan volume. These are used when adversary aircraft are within 15 miles, and a quick reaction capability is required. With all Auto Acq modes, the pilot simply places the target aircraft inside a synthetic scan volume indication in the HUD and the radar will automatically generate a lock.

Loaded with four inert AIM-7 Sparrow captive carry missiles on its underfuselage mountings and a single inert AIM-9 training round on the left outboard wing pylon, this F-15C reefs into a sharp turn for the benefit of the camera. With external fuel tanks jettisoned, the Eagle can pull up to 9G without adversely affecting the missiles.
(*Gary Klett via Author*)

ENHANCED IDENTIFICATION

Identifying the enemy from long range has, and always will be, one of the most important aspects of any intercept. Without a positive ID, long-range missiles cannot be fired, and it becomes necessary to close within visual range to visually ID (VID) the target. Typically, by entering the visual fight, a good BVR interceptor like the F-15 is denied the ability to engage the target on terms that suit it. Knowing this, the F-15 was built with a variety of systems that permit electronic identification of the target from long range. An electronic Identification Friend or Foe (IFF) system forms part of that capability, but the key technology employed is Non Cooperative Target Recognition (NCTR) – a classified but, paradoxically, well-known capability that underpinned nearly all of the F-15 kills that you will read about in this book.

In basic terms, NCTR compares radar returns from the target's fan and turbine blades with those stored in an on-board library. As radar waves bounce off of these blades, they carry with them a signature that can be compared to those stored in the library, allowing the threat type to be accurately identified. Once the radar has identified the aircraft type in a process that is 'almost instantaneous', it displays the information on the radar screen for the pilot to see – 'MiG-21', 'MiG-25', 'MiG-29', 'Mirage' etc. Of course, for NCTR to be effective, the F-15 must be able to see down the inlet or exhaust nozzles of the target. It may not work, therefore, when the target's aspect relative to the Eagle is too great.

NCTR proved so vital in allowing the early identification of radar contacts that it was actually part of the multi-tiered ROE matrix that pilots had to satisfy before a BVR shot could be taken in 1991. Whilst it is true that IFF and electronic listening platforms (such as the RC-135) also formed part of the enhance identification (EID) process, it is apparent that NCTR has been the real 'enabler' in most of the USAF's F-15 kills to date. NCTR is alluded to frequently in the passages that follow, but is rarely discussed overtly or explicitly.

KAL SHOOT DOWN AND RSAF KILLS

adena Air Base (AB), on the Japanese island of Okinawa, was home to the 12th TFS/18th TFW at the time Korean Airlines Boeing 747 flight KAL 007 went missing en route from the Alaskan capital of Anchorage to Seoul, South Korea, on 1 September 1983. As the world anticipated the worst possible news, US intelligence agencies already knew what had happened to the airliner. It had been shot down by a Soviet Su-15 interceptor after straying off course and overflying Sakhalin Island. None of the 269 passengers and crew on board the airliner survived.

Highly classified radio intercepts had recorded a Soviet ground controller directing a fighter to intercept the 747 after it had accidentally strayed into sovereign Soviet airspace. Believing that it might be a USAF RC-135 *Rivet Joint*, the pilot had been vectored to within very close proximity of KAL 007. He had radioed back that the contact was not a reconnaissance aircraft but a civil airliner, and he was then instructed to shoot it down – no warnings were issued to the crew, despite the Soviets later claiming that they had.

A race immediately began to be the first to recover the airliner's black box data- and voice-recorders from the scene of the crash. At this early stage, the US saw these as key to disproving Soviet claims that they had thought the aircraft was a reconnaissance platform flying without its lights on, and that the fighter which eventually shot it down had fired warning shots past the cockpit windows. Recovery of data from the black box was important because the classified radio intercepts could not be publicly disclosed until much later due to the covert way in which they had been obtained. The data recorders were the only means of unequivocally establishing the events of that night.

Seen in more recent years, two 18th FW Eagles arrive back at Kadena AB, Japan, following a sortie out over the Pacific. (*USAF*)

13

Heading the US effort to locate the recorders were unarmed US Navy P-3C Orion patrol aircraft from VP-4 and VP-40. These would need protection from marauding Soviet fighters, even though the wreckage of KAL 007 had fallen into international waters within the Sea of Japan. Select pilots from the 12th TFS at Kadena were therefore mobilised on 1 September to deploy with their brand-new F-15Cs to Misawa AB, on the tip of Honshu Island. Misawa was just 200 miles from Soviet-controlled Sakhalin Island, where US military intelligence estimated the airliner had been engaged.

Lt Rob Graeter was one of those selected to man the alert F-15s at Misawa. He recalled:

'We had a south CAP (Combat Air Patrol) and a north CAP. The southern CAP was abeam and to the west of Sapporo, on the northern island of Hokkaido. The north CAP was about 80 miles from the search area, and was closer to the tip of Hokkaido. We were flying with three "bags" (fuel tanks) and eight missiles (four AIM-9Ls and four AIM-7Fs), so we were not going to go any faster than Mach 1.1. What that meant was that we were about 20 minutes' flying time away from the northern CAP – maybe a little less if we really pushed it.'

There were ample F-15 and aerial tanker assets in the area to allow the Eagles to maintain a 24-hour airborne presence closer to the crash scene (Kadena was home to three fully equipped Eagle squadrons), but political tensions were deemed to be so strained that such a move would have been seen as provocative. Instead, the pilots and their six Eagles stood 24-hour alerts, waiting for the order to launch in response to hostile or threatening Soviet behaviour.

The Soviets hastily mobilised their own assets to recover the recorders, the search for which was centred southeast of Sakhalin. There were three Soviet fighter bases on the island – Smirynkh, Dolinsk-Sokol, and Yuzhno-Sakhalinsk – which were home to MiG-21s, MiG-23s and long-range MiG-31 'Foxhounds' (the latter

This Boeing 747-230B is identical to the one which was downed by an Su-15 interceptor on 1 September 1983. All 269 passengers and crew perished in the incident, and although unaware of it at the time, the Soviet radar controllers that had ordered the airliner's destruction were being eavesdropped by American intelligence gathering facilities in the region. (*Eduard Marmet via Author*)

Two 18th FW F-15C Eagles formate over Kadena in the late 1990s. The load out seen in this image is similar to that carried by Lt Graeter and his colleagues over a decade before when protecting P-3s searching the area where flight KAL 007 had been downed. In September 1983, the Eagles were loaded with four AIM-9 Sidewinders and four AIM-7 Sparrows, as well as three external fuel tanks. (*USAF*)

was a derivative of the MiG-25 'Foxbat'). The 'Foxhound' posed the greatest concern, and, in a case of *deja vu*, the USAF was once again unsure of how to deal with it. The MiG-31 had only recently been introduced to service, and was still largely enigmatic.

Then a junior lieutenant on his first F-15 assignment, Graeter remembers:

'The MIG-31s had just deployed to Yuzhno-Sakhalinsk, and we had intelligence reports telling us that one had made a run from Vladivostok to Sakhalin at 70,000 ft and Mach 2.3. They told us that his load out was two radar missiles and four infrared (IR) missiles. It was pretty eye-opening to know that he had enough gas to make that run *and* carry his missiles.'

As US Navy Orions combed the sea for any sign of the 747's black boxes, they came under increasing harassment from Soviet MiG-23s. Indeed, one pilot was so aggressive that he bumped wings with the unarmed aircraft. This, coupled with reports that bodies from the airliner were beginning to wash up on the beaches of outlying Japanese islands, was the final straw. On the third day of the search, as the P-3s made their way to the debris field, a MiG was detected launching. In response, Graeter and his CO, Roger Taylor, were scrambled.

'We started talking to AWACS and quickly detected a MiG-31 heading away from us and running northeast to southwest – Sakhalin to Vladivostok – probably 90 miles away. We climbed up in altitude in order to prepare to do something about him should he turn around and head towards the AWACS, which was northwest of Misawa.'

But the MiG passed to the east without incident.

The high-altitude, high-speed threat posed by the 'Foxbat' and 'Foxhound' required the employment of special tactics if they were to be dealt with effectively. Graeter explained:

'We had trained for the high-fast-flyer threat (MiG-25) and knew that to handle that guy we'd have to dump all of our fuel tanks. We would fly a profile that involved getting to 40,000 ft, then unload the jet (pushing forward on the stick to induce 0g) in full afterburner to get it to accelerate. Once up to Mach 1.7 or so, we'd gingerly pull the nose back up to 20–30 degrees, centre up the dot on the AIM-7 (align the nose with the computer-generated steering dot) and salvo all four missiles.'

It never came to that, though. Graeter and his colleagues launched a total of 12 sorties in the days that followed, and the sequence of events was always the same – the P-3s would roll back

Wearing the markings that adorned 18th TFW Eagles at the time of the KAL 007 incident, a 44th TFS F-15C taxies past the Kadena AB tower in the mid-1980s. This aircraft remains in service with the wing today. (*Robbie Shaw*)

A 67th TFS F-15C rolls out along the runway at Kadena AB in early 1983. Delivered to the 18th TFW in August 1979, this aircraft was transferred to the Oregon Air National Guard's 114th FS in May 2000. It is presently serving with the 57th Wing's 433rd Weapons School at Nellis AFB. (*USAF*)

It was the race to find KAL 007's black box and cockpit voice recorder that prompted the US Navy to deploy vulnerable P-3C Orions from VP-4 and VP-40 to search for the devices. F-15C pilot Lt Graeter later reflected that the true purpose of his brief deployment to Misawa had perhaps been to protect not the Orions, but the AWACS maintaining a permanent vigil in the skies above. This particular P-3C was operated by VP-40 'Marlins' during the crisis, the unit being assigned to Patrol and Reconnaissance Wing 10 at Moffett Field, California. (*Lockheed*)

The Royal Saudi Air Force received its first F-15 Eagles in 1983, little more than one year prior to them seeing combat for the first time against F-4E Phantom IIs of the Islamic Republic of Iran Air Force. (*Ian Black via Author*)

away from the MiGs, the F-15s would launch, the MiGs would be advised that Eagles were airborne, and they would immediately turn 180 degrees and head for home. The USAF pilots could see the 'Floggers', 'Fishbeds' and 'Foxhounds' on radar, often less than 80 miles distant, but AWACS always denied them permission to engage. Within a week the Soviets stopped harassing the recovery force, and within six weeks the Eagles had returned home. Although not a single shot had been fired, the F-15 had intimidated the Soviet fighter presence into submission. America's Eagles had passed their first test.

ROYAL SAUDI AIR FORCE EAGLES

The Royal Saudi Air Force (RSAF) purchased 46 F-15Cs (minus some of the TEWS elements and various sensitive radar modes) and 16 F-15Ds in 1983 under the Foreign Military Sales programme *Peace Sun*. The purchase followed a concerted effort by the Saudi monarchy to close a perceived gap in capabilities that they thought existed between the RSAF and the Islamic Republic of Iran Air Force (IRIAF).

Four years earlier, the Shah of Iran had been overthrown in a dramatic coup and replaced by a fanatical religious leadership whose intentions could not be trusted. To add to Saudi Arabia's woes, the Iranians had taken delivery of 79 F-14A Tomcats, and the jet's long-range AIM-54/AWG-9 weapon system, from 1976 onwards. The RSAF had initially considered the F-14 too, but opted to buy five E-3A AWACS (delivered in 1982) and F-15s instead.

There were serious political considerations resulting from *Peace Sun* that the US government had to consider, not least of which was the reaction the sale was bound to have elicited from the ever watchful Israelis. In order to minimise those tensions, RSAF Eagles were degraded to make them less capable, particularly against US-manufactured avionics and weapons systems.

An additional 24 jets were rushed to the RSAF from USAFE units in late 1990 in response to Operation *Desert Shield* (see Chapter 3).

FIRST KILL

The RSAF's first kill with the F-15 came amidst heightened tensions with Iran, and was conducted in the most extraordinary manner. Indeed, controversy surrounds the incident to this very day

On 5 June 1984, an IRIAF P-3F Orion detected merchant ships sailing along the Saudi side of the Persian Gulf, south of Lavan Island.

The Iranians had been waging a war of attrition against Iraqi oil tankers as part of the Iran–Iraq conflict, and the IRIAF had now been ordered to attack vessels trading through Saudi Arabian and Kuwaiti ports too – both countries were covertly supporting Iraq in the war against Iran.

Two IRIAF F-4E Phantom IIs from TFB 6 (61st TFW) were scrambled to attack the vessels, only to be detected soon after taking off by a USAF E-3 AWACS operating out of Saudi Arabia. Meanwhile, two RSAF Eagles (one F-15C and one F-15D) from No 6 Sqn were already airborne conducting a training flight with a USAF KC-10A Extender tanker. Aware that the merchant shipping was in imminent danger, the AWACS controller instructed the Eagles to leave the tanker track and vectored them towards the menacing F-4s (see *Osprey Combat Aircraft 37 - Iranian F-4 Phantom II Units in Combat*).

Getting the RSAF Eagle pilots to intercept F-4Es was no mean feat. It is believed that the controllers on board the AWACS had to plead with the Eagle pilots to do as they asked. Indeed, it was only after USAF instructor Capt Bill Tippin, sat in the back seat of the F-15D, encouraged the Saudis to go for the intercept that they accepted the tasking. As the F-4Es neared the Saudi island of al-Arabia – some 48 miles north of al-Jubayl naval base – on a southerly heading, the two Eagles engaged them head-on.

Under Tippin's guidance, and taking vectors from a Saudi officer on board the AWACS, the Eagle pilots finally obtained radar locks that allowed each to fire an AIM-7 Sparrow. Both missiles guided, downing one F-4E in a huge explosion and severely damaging the other. The latter aircraft limped away heavily damaged, but its pilot managed to land at an emergency airstrip on what is today the Iranian holiday resort of Kish Island.

The crew of the lost F-4, 1Lts Hamayoun Hekmati and Seyed-Cyrus Karimi, did not attempt to eject and perished in the explosion.

Following the interception of radio traffic between the F-15s and the AWACS, Iran later claimed – logically – that the pilots aboard the two Eagles were not Saudis, but Americans. The incident has never fully been explained by either the Saudi or US governments, but one has to wonder whether Capt Bill Tippin may have had a greater role to play in the engagement than has actually been conceded. Speculation that Tippin may have actually been flying the F-15D during the engagement could indeed be correct, although there is no way of actually releasing ordnance from the back seat of the D-model, leaving little doubt that it could only have been the front seat pilot who actually fired the AIM-7 that scored the kill.

This RSAF F-15D is similar to the one in which USAF Capt Bill Tippin was instructing air-to-air refuelling techniques when the call from AWACS came to intercept two IRIAF F-4E Phantom IIs on 5 June 1984. (*Ian Black via Author*)

OPERATION *DESERT STORM* KILLS

On 19 January 1991, the RSAF scored its second and third kills

Capt Ayehid Salah al-Shamrani of the RSAF's No 13 Sqn claimed two Iraqi Mirage F 1EQs destroyed on 19 March 1991. (*USAF*)

The two RSAF kills in Operation *Desert Storm* were almost certainly engineered to meet political agendas and expectations. Rumours surrounding the exact events that led to the kills are numerous and diverse, but there is a common thread within each story that, if true, does little to further the image of the RSAF. Here, a Saudi government official gives a press briefing on the F-15's operations with No 13 Sqn at Dhahran during Operation *Desert Shield*. (*Ian Black via Author*)

with the F-15 when Capt Ayehid Salah al-Shamrani of No 13 Sqn engaged and destroyed two Iraqi Air Force (IrAF) Mirage F 1EQs during Operation *Desert Storm* (see Chapter 3). Details of the engagement are sketchy, but US sources have told the author that Salah was vectored towards the Mirages soon after they were detected taking off and heading for coalition naval vessels in the Persian Gulf.

Reports indicate that a USAF AWACS provided the RSAF Eagle with good vectors but, allegedly, Salah struggled to complete the intercept. Running desperately short of time before the Mirages brought the naval vessels within striking distance of their anti-ship Exocet missiles, Salah was talked, step-by-step, into position behind the French-made fighters. He eventually employed two AIM-9Ps, both of which guided squarely to their targets. One former F-15 pilot observed:

'There are several very valid questions to ask about these kills. Firstly, why is the pilot of an aircraft designed to kill BVR doing a stern conversion to visual range without firing a shot? Secondly, where was his wingman during all this? Thirdly, he fired both missiles while they were still "caged", if I remember correctly.'

'Uncaging' the seeker from the radar before firing was standard practice, as it allowed the pilot to validate that the seeker was tracking the target. Failing to 'uncage' was considered to be something of a *faux pas* within the fighter pilot community.

Unsurprisingly, RSAF F-15s were kept well away from the 'coalface' during *Desert Storm*, flying what were termed 'Goalie CAPs' for the duration of the war. 'Goalie CAPs' were placed some distance behind the Iraq/Saudi border, effectively putting the RSAF Eagles in a position where they could not interfere with the efforts of the rest of the Coalition.

Whilst one USAF pilot who flew an exchange tour with the RSAF in the 1990s told the author that two particular Saudi F-15 pilots were the best Eagle pilots that he had ever met', the overall level of professionalism, ability and pride amongst the RSAF is reportedly mediocre at best.

It is almost certain that these two Mirage kills were driven by a political directive that was designed to draw an Arab nation into the limelight. There is certainly circumstantial evidence to support this theory, not least of which was the close proximity of US Navy F-14 Tomcats, which were said to have been in an equally good position to engage the Mirages, and could have done so in a more timely and competent manner. Existing reports suggest that the F 1s came within minutes of being able to engage their targets before they were downed.

COLOUR PLATES

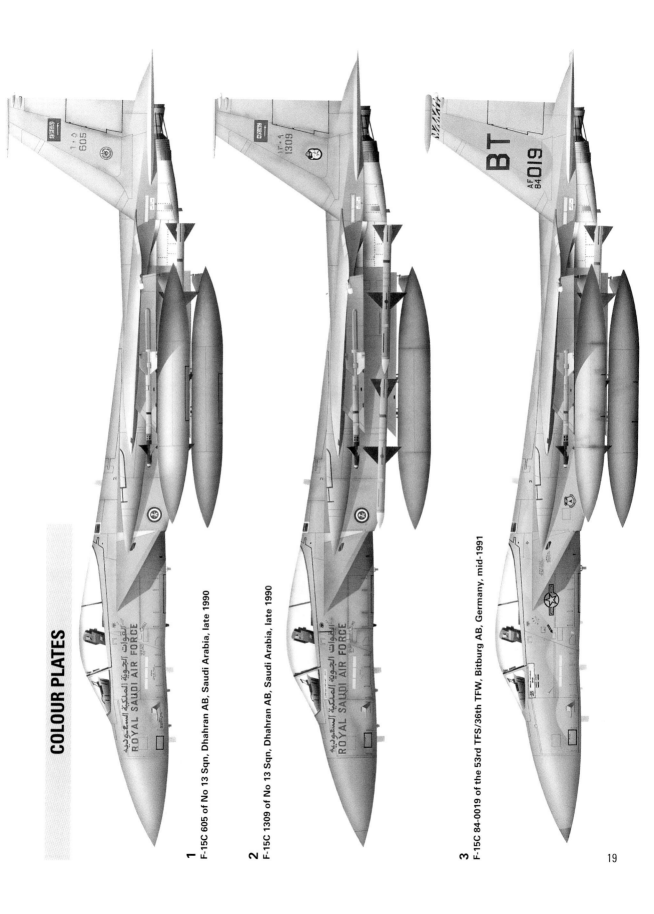

1
F-15C 605 of No 13 Sqn, Dhahran AB, Saudi Arabia, late 1990

2
F-15C 1309 of No 13 Sqn, Dhahran AB, Saudi Arabia, late 1990

3
F-15C 84-0019 of the 53rd TFS/36th TFW, Bitburg AB, Germany, mid-1991

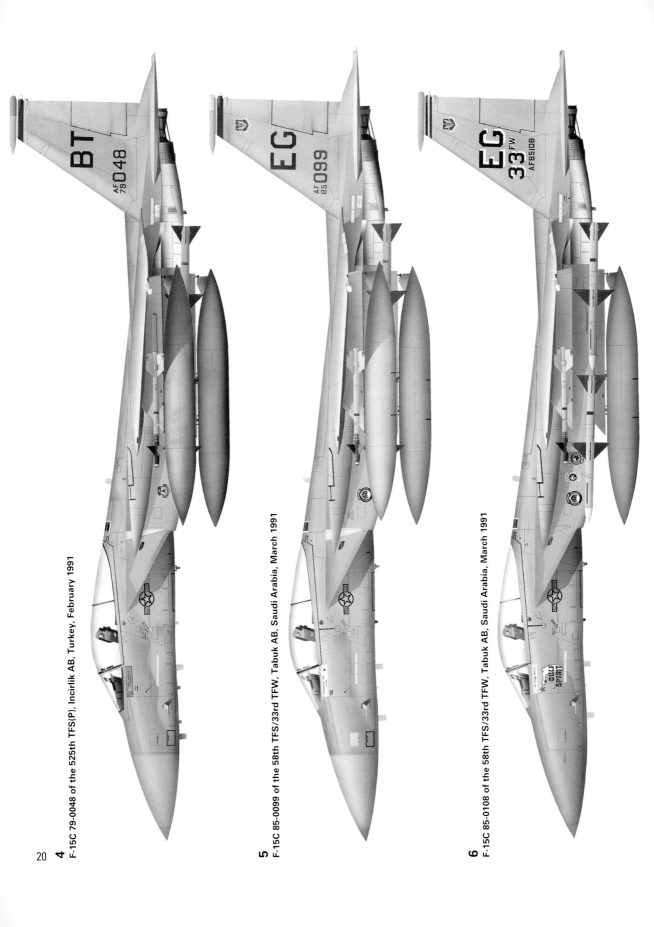

4

F-15C 79-0048 of the 525th TFS(P), Incirlik AB, Turkey, February 1991

5

F-15C 85-0099 of the 58th TFS/33rd TFW, Tabuk AB, Saudi Arabia, March 1991

6

F-15C 85-0108 of the 58th TFS/33rd TFW, Tabuk AB, Saudi Arabia, March 1991

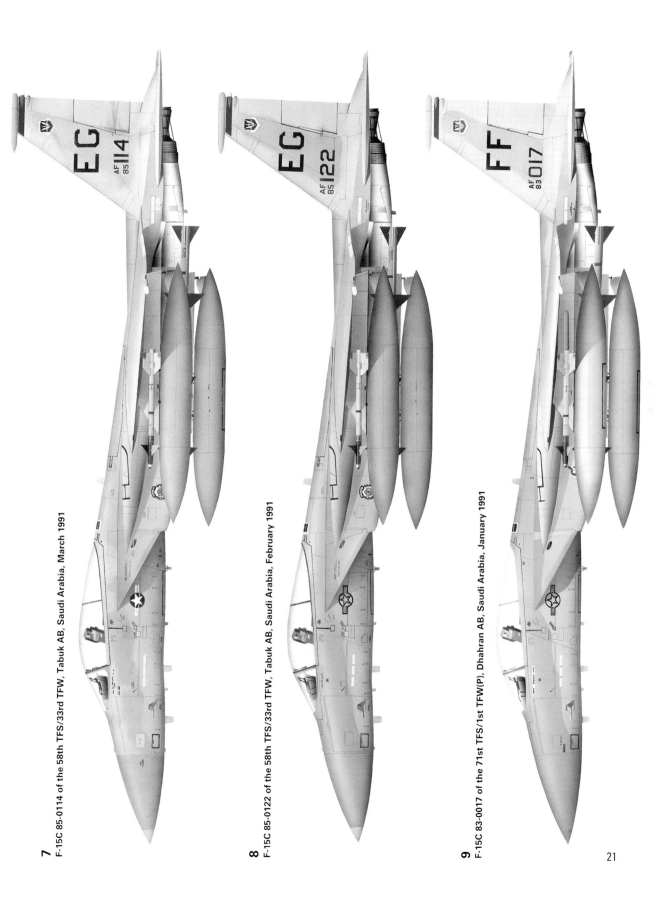

7
F-15C 85-0114 of the 58th TFS/33rd TFW, Tabuk AB, Saudi Arabia, March 1991

8
F-15C 85-0122 of the 58th TFS/33rd TFW, Tabuk AB, Saudi Arabia, February 1991

9
F-15C 83-0017 of the 71st TFS/1st TFW(P), Dhahran AB, Saudi Arabia, January 1991

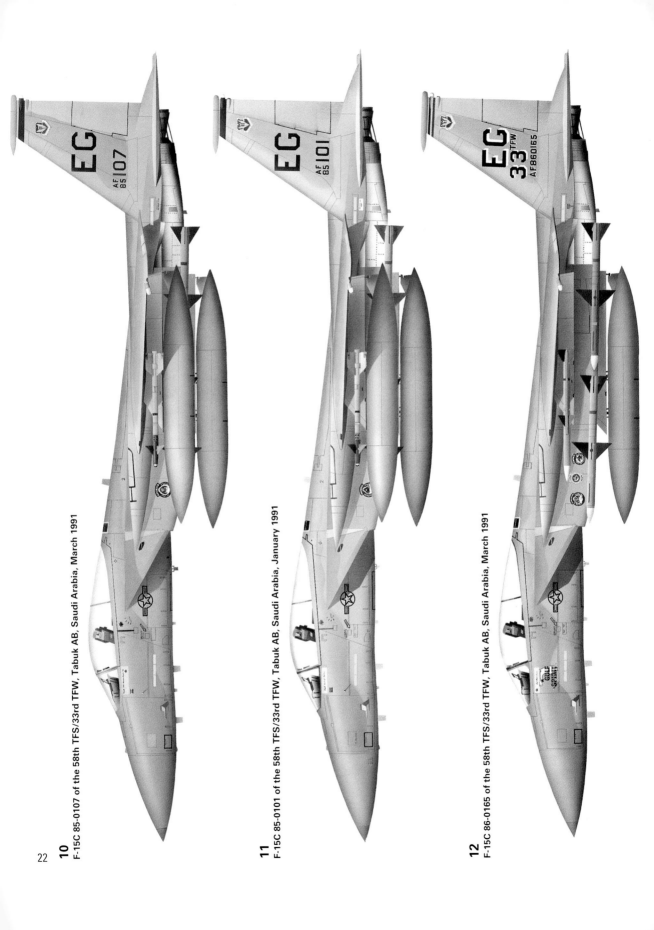

10
F-15C 85-0107 of the 58th TFS/33rd TFW, Tabuk AB, Saudi Arabia, March 1991

11
F-15C 85-0101 of the 58th TFS/33rd TFW, Tabuk AB, Saudi Arabia, January 1991

12
F-15C 86-0165 of the 58th TFS/33rd TFW, Tabuk AB, Saudi Arabia, March 1991

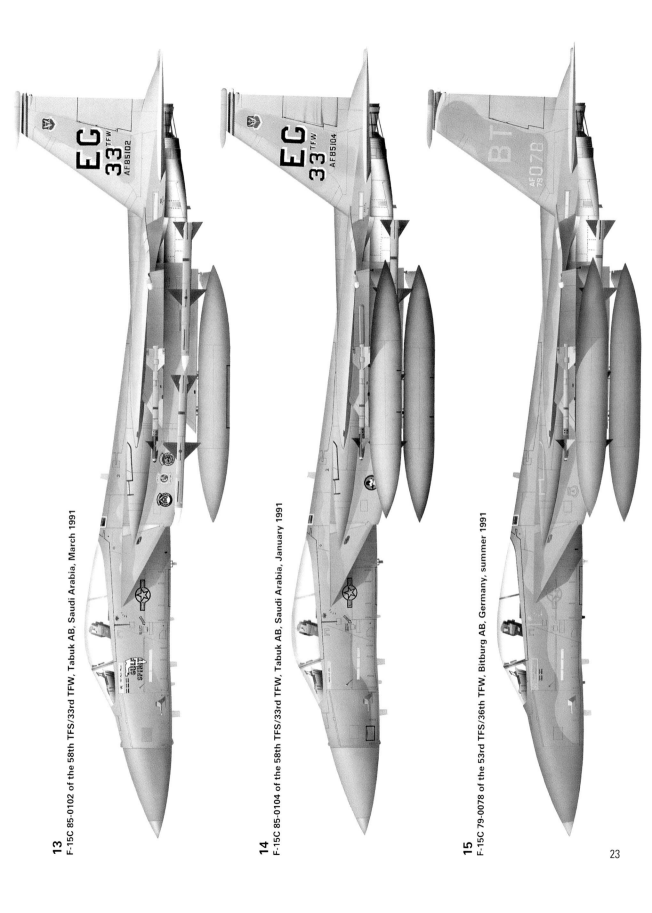

13
F-15C 85-0102 of the 58th TFS/33rd TFW, Tabuk AB, Saudi Arabia, March 1991

14
F-15C 85-0104 of the 58th TFS/33rd TFW, Tabuk AB, Saudi Arabia, January 1991

15
F-15C 79-0078 of the 53rd TFS/36th TFW, Bitburg AB, Germany, summer 1991

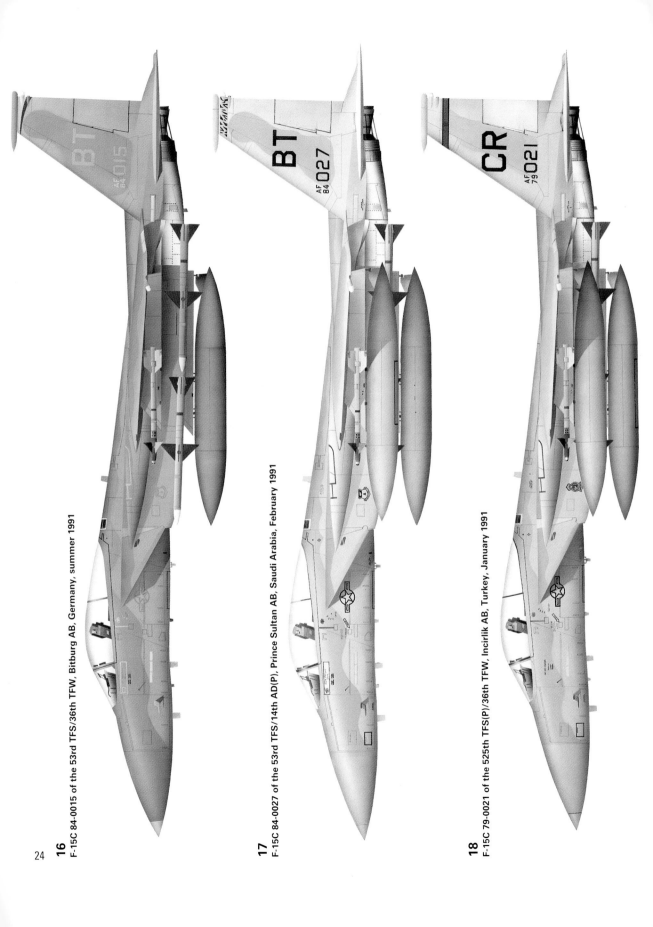

16
F-15C 84-0015 of the 53rd TFS/36th TFW, Bitburg AB, Germany, summer 1991

17
F-15C 84-0027 of the 53rd TFS/14th AD(P), Prince Sultan AB, Saudi Arabia, February 1991

18
F-15C 79-0021 of the 525th TFS(P)/36th TFW, Incirlik AB, Turkey, January 1991

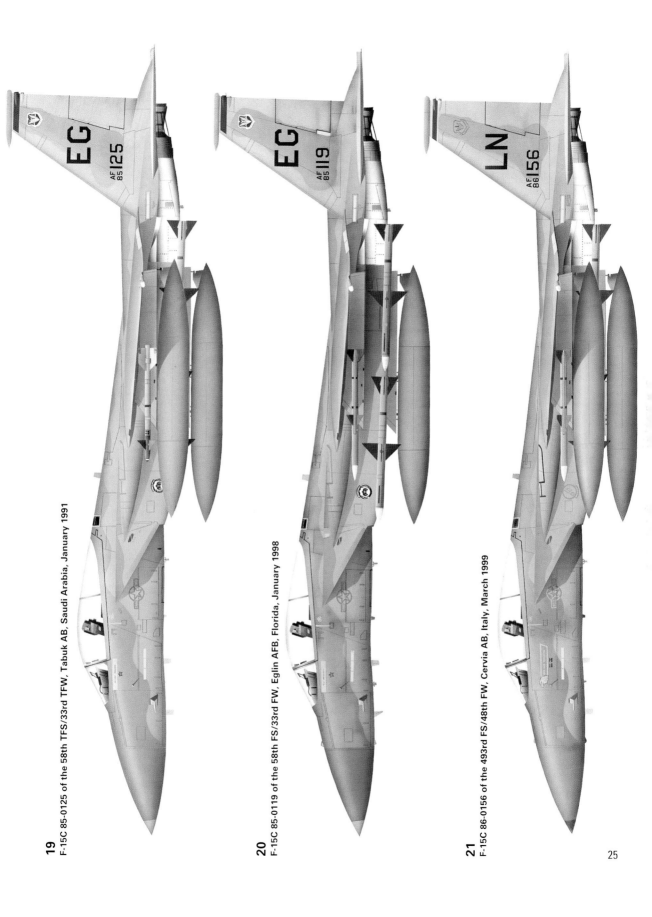

19

F-15C 85-0125 of the 58th TFS/33rd TFW, Tabuk AB, Saudi Arabia, January 1991

20

F-15C 85-0119 of the 58th FS/33rd FW, Eglin AFB, Florida, January 1998

21

F-15C 86-0156 of the 493rd FS/48th FW, Cervia AB, Italy, March 1999

25

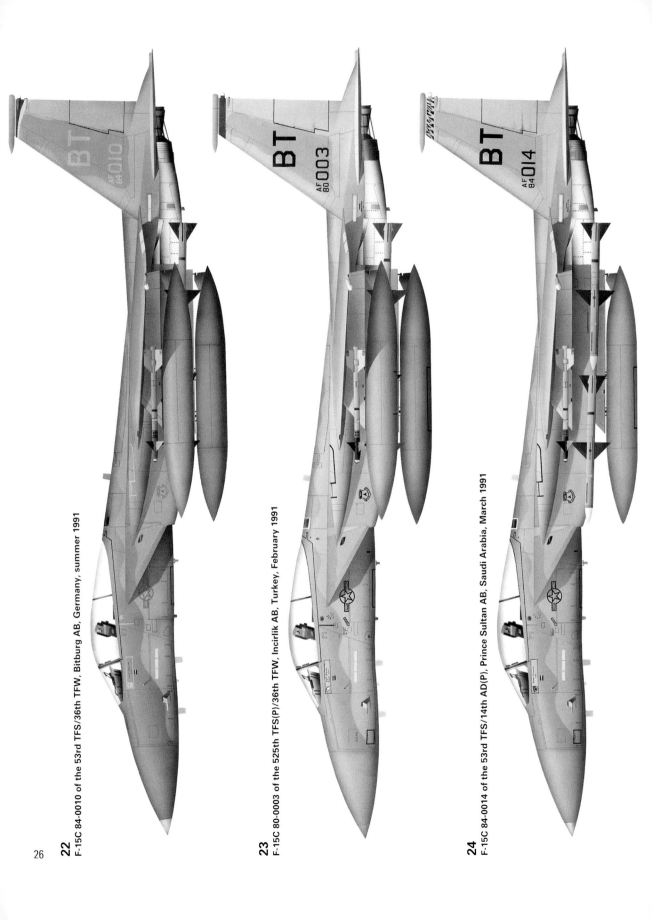

22
F-15C 84-0010 of the 53rd TFS/36th TFW, Bitburg AB, Germany, summer 1991

23
F-15C 80-0003 of the 525th TFS(P)/36th TFW, Incirlik AB, Turkey, February 1991

24
F-15C 84-0014 of the 53rd TFS/14th AD(P), Prince Sultan AB, Saudi Arabia, March 1991

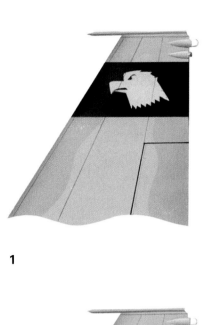

1

2

3

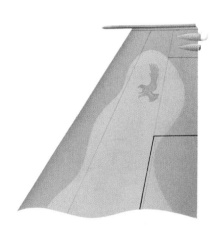

4

5

6

DUCKS IN A BARREL

On 2 August 1990, Iraq acted upon its historical claim to the small oil-rich country of Kuwait. Its dictator, Saddam Hussein, had massed a large invasion force north of the Kuwaiti border, and Kuwait was unprepared for the *blitzkrieg* attack that followed. Iraqi armour and infantry, supported by helicopter gunships, entered the country with minimal resistance. The international community's initial military response, christened Operation *Desert Shield*, was defensive in nature. On Thursday, 17 January 1991, this defensive posture gave way to Operation *Desert Storm*. Where *Shield* had allowed Coalition forces to amass whilst diplomacy took its course, *Storm* was the US-led coalition effort that would expeditiously decimate the Iraqi invaders and rid Kuwait of its occupying forces.

At the centre of it all was the F-15C, initially patrolling the skies and safeguarding the Coalition build-up, then clearing the way for allied aircraft to operate with almost complete immunity from the IrAF.

DEPLOYMENTS AND ORDER OF BATTLE

The F-15 was the first aircraft mobilised when news of the Iraqi invasion reached then US President, George Bush Snr. The 1st TFW at Langley AFB, Virginia, was immediately put on standby to rapid-deploy in a move intended to curb any attempts by Iraq to attack Saudi Arabia. Some 24 F-15Cs and three F-15Ds from the 71st TFS arrived fully armed at Dhahran AB, Saudi Arabia, on 7 August, where

The 1st TFW – the oldest fighter wing in the USAF – was the first Coalition unit to deploy to the Gulf region for Operation *Desert Shield*, the unit sending 27 F-15C/Ds from the 71st TFS to Dhahran on 7 August 1990. One of the 24 F-15CS despatched on that date was this particular aircraft, 81-0035, seen here bearing the colours of the 27th TFS in the 1980s. The jet remains with 1st FW today, having served exclusively with the wing since its delivery to the USAF on 30 November 1982. (*USAF*)

Following hot on the heels of the boys from Langley, Eglin AFB despatched the 58th TFS from the 33rd TFW. The squadron was exclusively equipped with F-15Cs fitted with the APG-63(V)0 radar. The 60th TFS supplemented the unit's strength by contributing an even mix of aircraft using the (V)0 and APG-70 radar sets. These 58th TFS jets are seen in later years, the squadron's nickname – 'The Gorillas' – clearly visible in white on their tail flashes. (*Gary Klett via Author*)

Keen to sample the action, the USAFE managed to massage its way into the operational gameplan being created in Riyadh. Bitburg AB, Germany, deployed the 53rd and 525th TFSs, and the former drew the short straw and was sent to Saudi Arabia under CENTCOM control, while the latter went to Turkey and remained under USAFE 'ownership'. This particular jet is seen wearing 53rd TFS markings in the late 1980s. By the time it deployed to the war it was a 525th TFS machine. (*Ian Black via Author*)

they operated under the revised title of the 1st TFW (Provisional), 14th Air Division (Provisional). The aircraft immediately started flying CAPs along the border between Saudi Arabia and Iraq. The next day, an additional 25 F-15C/Ds from the 27th TFS arrived, marking the deployment of 52 1st TFW Eagles in just 48 hours!

Later that same month a further 24 F-15Cs and 36 pilots deployed from the 58th TFS (augmented by crews and aircraft from the 60th TFS), 33rd TFW, based at Eglin AFB in Florida. They were sent to King Faisal AB (a RSAF F-5 base also known as Tabuk AB) in the far northwestern corner of Saudi Arabia in an effort to spread the placement of Eagles along the border. Col Larry Pitts was one of the pilots to fly a 33rd TFW jet from Florida to Saudi Arabia. He recalled:

'We flew as four six-ships non-stop from Eglin to Saudi Arabia, and it took about 15.5 flying hours and seven aerial refuellings to complete the deployment. We were quite a way from the Saudi border (although the closest F-15 unit to Baghdad), which was not ideal because we had to take off and fly for an hour before we even got to our tanker. Only then could we think about turning north and actually doing our mission. During the course of the war we routinely flew 10-hour+ missions as a consequence of that.'

The 36th TFW at Bitburg AB, Germany, was earmarked to send its 24 53rd TFS MSIP II F-15Cs to Prince Sultan AB (nicknamed 'PSAB'), again in Saudi Arabia, where they would also come under the operational control of the 14th Air Division (Provisional), Central Command. The 53rd TFS's Col Jay Denney recalled:

'We knew we were on tap to deploy from October 1990. When Iraq invaded Kuwait on 2 August we were at Soesterberg AB, in Holland, participating in the *William Tell* exercise (an annual USAF-sponsored mock air-to-air combat event). Eglin and Langley both deployed, and on 6 August

we were told to return home to get ready to go. We eventually arrived at "PSAB" on 20 December and started flying CAP right away.'

Not wishing to appear superfluous to requirements, USAF Europe (USAFE) managed to convince supreme Coalition commander, Gen Norman Schwarzkopf, that it should also send F-15Cs to the region to assist 'under its own command'. Schwarzkopf conceded, allowing Bitburg's remaining squadron – the 525th TFS – to deploy under USAFE control to Incirlik AB, in Turkey. The 525th TFS was to patrol Iraq's northern territories, but only on the condition that it did not interfere with the plans Schwarzkopf had already laid down for the air war. Single aircraft from both the 22nd and 32nd TFSs at Soesterberg were borrowed by the 525th TFS in order to help make up the numbers. Still more F-15Cs from the 32nd TFS joined the Turkish-based 525th TFS on the first day of the war – 17 January 1991.

Seen here conducting dissimilar air combat training with a RAF Hawk T 1A trainer, two Soesterberg F-15Cs form on their leader. Soesterberg's 32nd TFS Eagles and pilots participated as part of the 525th TFS(P) from Bitburg, and members of both squadrons spent the war enjoying the relative luxury afforded to them at Incirlik AB, Turkey. (*Ian Black via Author*)

IrAF ORDER OF BATTLE

On paper, the Iraqi air threat was portentous. Saddam Hussein had invested vast sums of money equipping the IrAF with a mix of modern Soviet- and French-made combat aircraft that were capable of fighting for air supremacy, repelling ground-based assaults and attacking strategic targets. Aircraft were assigned to five major IrAF command bodies – Transport Command, with two or three squadrons operating several composite flights, Training Command, consisting of around ten flying schools, the Army-controlled Aviation Corps, with seven wings (one for each Army Corps), each of which had four composite squadrons, and Air Defence and Air Support Commands, which operated Iraq's most potent aircraft types.

A wing of Mirage F 1EQs, totalling eight squadrons, was controlled both by Air Defence Command (ADC) and Air Support Command (ASC). Each of these units was equipped with approximately seven or less flyable jets. The Mirage posed a considerable threat in a BVR engagement on account of its Matra 530D radar-guided missiles. Indeed, the thought of any IrAF fighter getting in amongst a Coalition strike package caused more than a few sleepless nights. ASC also maintained ten brigades equipped with Su-20/22 'Fitters', MiG-23BN/BK/MS 'Floggers' and ancient Hawker Hunters, all of which were under-strength and incapable of attaining anything like the sortie generation rates of Coalition squadrons.

Although the F 1EQs rightly caused much concern in Coalition ranks, a greater threat was posed by ADC's five brigades of MiG-21 'Fishbeds', air-to-air MiG-23 'Floggers', MiG-25 'Foxbats' and the formidable MiG-29 'Fulcrum'. The 'Foxbats' operated as part of a

F-15C pilots knew that merging with a MiG-29 'Fulcrum' could be very bad for their health, and not surprisingly, standard doctrine saw each intercept make maximum use of the Eagle's BVR prowess. But, as time soon showed, avoiding the merge was not always possible, least of all when the IrAF used initiative and cunning to execute the fight on their own terms. Note the 'Fulcrum's' smoky engines (centre). (*USAF*)

This IrAF MiG-23ML 'Flogger' was photographed while being refurbished in the former USSR. The Iraqis attempted to use MiG-23s in cooperation with MiG-29s, but dropped this idea after a MiG-23 was shot down by its leader on the first night of the war. Russian and Ukrainian sources claim that IrAF MiG-23MLs were responsible for the destruction of an Italian Tornado IDS, shot down over southern central Iraq on the second night of the war. (*Tom Cooper Collection via Author*)

composite interceptor-reconnaissance wing, with four squadrons boasting a mixed force of MiG-25Ps and RBs. Crews flying these aircraft would undoubtedly attempt to target High Value Asset (HVA) platforms.

The MiG-29 posed the greatest BVR threat, though, as it could employ the semi-active radar-homing (SARH) R-27 medium-range missile. However, its radar was not optimised for a long-range fight, and it was very poor in the look-down/shoot-down scenario. Once at the merge, the tables could turn in the MiG's favour, as it was highly manoeuvrable and could fire its short-range IR missiles high off-boresight with the aid of a helmet-mounted monocle sight. The jet also featured a passive Infra Red Search and Track optical sensor in a fairing on the nose with which to stealthily pick out targets undetected.

Finally, the IrAF possessed a composite wing made up of three Tu-22 'Blinder' units, a Tu-16/H-6D 'Badger' squadron and two Su-24MK 'Fencer' squadrons, both of which were in the process of transitioning to the high-performance bomber. The 'Fencer' was of the same ilk as the F-111, and had the capacity to mount devastating attacks against ground and sea targets.

IrAF squadrons were spread across four Sector Commands, each of which was linked to an extensive Ground Control Intercept (GCI) and Integrated Air Defence System (IADS) network. The central control for the GCI and IADS network would employ aerial assets in accordance with the Soviet doctrine that they had been schooled in.

Despite superior training, tactics, and equipment, the USAF formed the view that it would probably lose a number of F-15s in aerial combat simply because a vast number of IrAF pilots had seen extensive action in the recent Iran–Iraq War. In contrast to the seasoned ranks of the IrAF, few pilots within the Eagle squadrons had seen any combat whatsoever. Official figures drawn from *SPEARTIP 014-90*, a formerly classified USAF/US Navy intelligence document titled 'Iraq Fighter-Interceptor Capabilities', show that the US believed the Iraqis to possess 35 MiG-29s (including six two-seaters), 34 Mirage F 1EQ-2/4/5/6s and six Mirage F 1EQ-7s, 22 MiG-23MLs, 22 MiG-25PDs (export) and PDSs, and 55 MiG-23MS/MF aircraft.

SPEARTIP 014-90 concluded that only the MiG-29 had an overland look-down/shoot-down capability, while the F 1EQ-5/5/6/7 possessed a similar capability only over water. The MiG-23ML had a limited depressed angle capability, but was able to employ the R-23/24 (AA-7) in the forward hemisphere. There was no confirmation that Iraq had received R-23/24T, R-40T and R-27T IR missiles, and the report noted that forward-quarter IR shots were 'believed to be unlikely'. Similarly, the Iraqis had captured some 60 Matra R 530 medium-range radar-guided missiles from Kuwait, but despite their all-aspect capability, Iraqi F 1EQ pilots were not trained to use them from the forward aspect.

The report went on to state that the IrAF pilots typically fired their medium-range missiles at maximum range – between ten and thirteen nautical miles. Iraqi fighters usually flew in a 'trail' formation of unknown separation, and mainly operated at medium altitude (they descended to low altitude only during daylight hours, and only in pursuit of an already identified and engaged target). MiG-23s were used for CAP and escort work, while MiG-25s and Mirages operated as interceptors.

In respect of electronic warfare (EW), the report stated that electronic counter-measures (ECM), chaff and flares and radar warning receivers (RWR) were never used offensively. Even though the availability of ECM was a 'go/no-go' decider for all Mirage, MiG-25, and Su-22 pilots, crews across the IrAF were poorly informed about their EW capabilities, and used their RWRs solely for survival purposes. Indeed, Osprey author Tom Cooper (a specialist in Middle Eastern air forces) stated that the IrAF's MiG-23BNs, MiG-23MSs and most of its MiG-21MFs had no RWR equipment installed at all.

The report said of the Iraqi pilots that they had an 'exaggerated fear of radar guided missiles', although given the pummelling they had received at the hands of Iranian F-14s and the AIM-54 Phoenix missile, this comment may well have been unfairly constructed. The report went on to say that a lock-on by any US fighter should result in the Iraqis jettisoning their drop tanks and returning to base post haste. However, if cornered, they would do their utmost to survive. 'Post-merge manoeuvring', the report's author wrote, would 'most likely' be to turn and run. Cooper commented that, 'It was their only tactic. If the first attack was not successful, the Iraqis would disengage. They conducted no rigorous air combat manoeuvring training, and were consequently not trained at all in dogfighting'.

SPEARTIP 014-90 summarised that the MiG-23, MiG-25 and MiG-29 pilots were especially dependent on GCI, despite the IrAF's GCI equipment being old, and slow to process data. In practice, this meant that any aggressive manoeuvring on the part of a US fighter would translate into a delay of 15 to 30 seconds before this information was registered and passed to Iraqi interceptors. In fact,

Ready to face the Iraqi threat, Bitburg Eagles from the 525th TFS(P) await the challenge ahead on the Incirlik ramp. USAF intelligence reports obtained since the war contained detailed information on Iraqi tactics, weapons systems and capabilities. Interestingly, it concluded – unfairly, in my view – that the average Iraqi pilot had an exaggerated fear of radar-guided missiles. (*Bob Hehemann via Author*)

Cooper added, 'the MiG-25 and the MiG-29 were completely dependent on the GCI, whose voice communications with the ground could be easily jammed'.

THE 'FRAG' AND *DESERT STORM*

On 17 January 1991, the order to execute the first strikes was given by President Bush – Operation *Desert Storm* had begun. The Air Tasking Order (ATO), which was referred to as the 'frag', and was basically the roadmap that charted each and every planned sortie, focused initially on killing the IADS that protected Iraq, and on taking out airfields, Hardened Aircraft Shelters (HAS), and aircraft. With this achieved, Iraqi armour, C3 (Command, Control and Communications) and logistics supplies could then be struck, leading to the rapid weakening of the enemy prior to a Coalition ground assault.

The first three days of the 'frag' were as scripted as possible, with changes occurring only to accommodate a fickle weather system that could generate generous blankets of cloud cover for days on end. The original ATO (as drafted soon after the 1st TFW deployed in August 1990) saw all F-15Cs providing escort and CAP from the south, but the decision to deploy USAFE F-15s to Turkey allowed planners to sandwich the IrAF by attacking it from the north as well.

From the moment they arrived in theatre, the USAF's Eagles flew CAP sorties south of the Saudi/Iraq border. While Eagles from Bitburg, Eglin and Langley operated at the forward edge of the protective umbrella, RSAF F-15s such as this one remained further south and acted as 'Goal Keepers' should an Iraqi strike aircraft slip though the net. (*Ian Black via Author*)

The three F-15 wings organised themselves in different ways. The 58th TFS/33rd TFW favoured a 'hard crew' approach that assigned a cadre of 12 pilots (three four-ships) to the offensive counter air (OCA) mission for the first ten days of the war, while the rest of the squadron's pilots performed defensive counter air (DCA) and High Value Asset CAP missions (HVACAP). HVACAP and DCA was typically about protecting tankers, AWACS, and reconnaissance assets which were orbiting south of the Saudi–Iraq border. OCA was, by contrast, an offensive mission that saw the F-15 push deep into Iraqi airspace.

The 'Gorillas', as the 58th TFS nicknamed themselves, had a surplus of Fighter Weapons School (FWS) graduates amongst its ranks, and was arguably the best-trained F-15 unit in the US Air Force at that time, having participated in the 1989 and 1990 *Red Flag* exercises that prepared pilots for war. Rick Tollini, who led the first F-15C sweep into

Iraq, commented that the unit had also worked with the secretive 422nd Test & Evaluation Squadron to develop high-level tactics.

Rather than assigning pilots according to mission category, the 71st TFS/1st TFW and 53rd TFS/4th TFW(P) adopted a night/day shift pattern that split the aircrew into two teams for the entire war. This offered the advantage that the night team could plan the next day mission while the day team slept, and vice versa.

In the events that unfolded during the first night of *Desert Storm*, the USAF scored six kills against the IrAF, all at the hands of the F-15C.

Day 1 of the ATO called for F-15s from the Bitburg, Langley and Eglin wings to patrol discrete areas of responsibility as defined by lines of longitude or recognisable geographical features. Capt Jon 'J B' Kelk, flying F-15C 85-0125, call-sign 'Pennzoil 63', was one of the 58th FS pilots sortied on the opening night of the war:

'There were eight F-15s from the 58th TFS at Tabuk assigned to patrol the western sector of Iraq. Bitburg's 53rd TFS at "PSAB" was supplying eight airframes to patrol the central zone and the 1st TFW at Dhahran was covering the very east of Iraq with four jets. We planned to march up the centre of our area and clean out the IrAF. If you take Baghdad and separate it into two halves, east and west, then we were taking the western sector, with particular attention given to the Iraqi airfields at H1, H2, Mudaysis, Al Assad, and Al Taqaddum. Our job was to dispense with the air threat within the western sector, while the Langley and Bitburg guys cleared the air east of Baghdad.'

In the early hours of 17 January 1991, the 58th TFS launched two flights of four F-15Cs, operating with the call-signs 'Citgo 61' to '64' and 'Pennzoil 61' to '64'. Capt Kelk recalled:

'I was the number three guy in "Pennzoil" flight, with Rick Tollini as flight lead. We were a paired four-ship, and the plan was that we would alternate the lead role every other night, so he would lead tonight and I would lead the next mission – both of us were FWS graduates, so it made sense to alternate the responsibility. Larry Pitts was in the number two jet and my number four was Mark Williams.'

The broad ATO plan for the first night was to use F-117s and F-15E Strike Eagles to make a surprise attack at 0300 hrs local, as Kelk explained:

'This was to take place over Baghdad and H2 and H3 airfields, where the Strike Eagles would engage in Scud missile hunting activities at low level, undetected. As they egressed, we were to take our aircraft and shoot down all the bad guys – a wall of our eight F-15C Eagles to mow down whoever took off from an Iraqi airfields in the area. So, you had the surprise attack, then us, then a follow-on attack consisting of everyone else.'

Focused and ready for war. Training immediately prior to 17 January 1991 was as intense as it could have been. Indeed, for several months F-15 pilots had patrolled Saudi Arabia's borders 24 hours a day. By the time war came, the Eagle community across Saudi Arabia and to the north in Turkey were psychologically and physically prepared for the challenge ahead. Their preparedness would serve them well. (*Ian Black via Author*)

Despite the plan's simplicity, it quickly came apart. Notwithstanding horrendous weather that presented some of the toughest air-to-air refuelling conditions the pilots had ever experienced – towering cumulonimbus up to 30,000 ft on a pitch-black, turbulent, night, and without any external lights – the IrAF learned of the F-15Es' 'surprise attack' through rudimentary intelligence assets, as Capt Kelk explained:

'The problem was that there were manned listening posts along the border where Iraqi soldiers listened for the sound of aircraft. A flight of 18 F-15Es makes a lot of noise!

'Shooting down one of your friends is a mortifying thought, and even though we had our own means of identifying a contact, and AWACS was there to help, it is a much better plan to keep "friendlies" and "hostiles" apart. The key component to the plan, therefore, was to let the F-117s and F-15Es clear out of the area. That way, when we went north into Iraq, we knew that anything in front of us was an enemy. However, at around 0305 hrs, AWACS called to tell us that it had detected Iraqis flying, which was a problem because we were still marshalling some 50 miles to the south of the Saudi–Iraq border, and "Citgo" flight, which planned to marshal up with us before the push towards Iraq, was about 100 miles behind us. We should have had plenty more time, but as soon as AWACS called, "Pennzoil" flight pushed north regardless.'

When the call came to push, Kelk was less than pleased at going into battle with 'friendlies' and enemies mixed into together ahead of him:

'I was thinking to myself, "So much for that great eight-ship wall!", but we had no choice but to deal with the hand we were dealt. We got set up at our assigned altitude (30,000 ft) and headed north.'

'Citgo' flight was further south of 'Pennzoil' because its leader, Rob Graeter, had decided to fly south of the poor weather. 'Pennzoil', which cycled onto the tanker as 'Citgo' departed to the south, may well have followed suit had the call not come from AWACS to push early. As the 'Pennzoil' two-ships turned north, the weather began to clear considerably. The flight assumed a lateral separation of around five miles, with each wingman displaced from his lead by another two miles. This nine-mile 'wall' formation was about to initiate the first contact of the war with the IrAF. Manning the F-15Cs from left to right were Pitts, Tollini, Kelk and Williams.

'Pennzoil' was directed by AWACS to engage two groups of bandits located northeast of Radif al Khafi Highway Strip and southeast of Mudaysis AB. Tollini and Pitts broke off to engage the western group, whilst Kelk and Williams were 'snapped' – given radar vectors by AWACS – to the eastern group. Larry Pitts, flying as Tollini's wingman on the far left of the formation, recalled that their worst nightmare had materialised:

'When I hit the (IFF) button to try and ID the guys out in front of me, I had 40 or 50 friendly returns come up on the radar scope. I chased down a single contact because it threatened a strike package, but he ran and eventually landed. Had I got into weapons firing parameters though, I'd have really had a hard time deciding whether to shoot – we really did not want to kill a "friendly".'

The 58th TFS was inundated with skillful and lucid flight leads who exuded talent. Rick 'Kluso' Tollini (above) was a Fighter Weapons School graduate, and he was leading the flight of four when John Kelk scored the first kill of the war. Larry 'Cherry' Pitts (top) was Tollini's section leader that night. Tollini is pictured on alert – replete with g-suit and kneeboard – playing the obligatory *Gameboy* for relaxation! (*Larry Pitts via Author*)

Fifty miles into Iraq, Kelk picked up enemy contacts on his radar:

'I got a spike (radar warning indication) that someone had locked onto me at about the same time as I locked onto him. Our formation was now "Pennzoil 1" and "2" in the west and "Pennzoil 3" and "4" in the east. My contact range was about 35 miles, and, to my knowledge, there was just the one guy out in front. As I pressed the attack, Williams stayed in radar sweep to check for other contacts. We had a thing called a Mode 4 rollover, where all the (encrypted) Mode 4 IFF codes changed at 0300 hrs. But what if a guy was doing other things then? What if he was trying to evade, drop bombs, forgot to change the code or move the switch? I didn't want to shoot down a guy just because he had forgotten to flick a switch, so I wanted to get an additional confirmation from AWACS.

'There was so much going on that the call was never completed, so I had to use my own on-board systems to determine that my target was not friendly. The bandit climbed from about 7000 ft to 17,000 ft, and was clearly manoeuvring in relation to me when I eventually took the shot. I was in an advantageous position at 30,000 ft because I could increase the range of my weapons against the lower-flying MiG.'

As Kelk closed on his target, Tollini and Pitts saw their group turn away and depart the area, allowing them to head back east to support their formation. Turning right towards Kelk and Williams, Tollini was also spiked momentarily by the lone target – an IrAF MiG-29.

As Kelk and the enemy jet hurtled towards each other at a combined speed of more than 1400 mph, the American pilot closed his eyes to protect his night vision and pressed the pickle button on his control stick, unleashing one of his four AIM-7M Sparrow air-to-air missiles. Simultaneously, he wrenched his F-15C into a high-G turn and enthusiastically mashed a button on his throttle to release chaff:

'I fired the missile from high altitude and at above the Mach, which gave me a decided advantage. I distinctly remember feeling the missile coming off – a 500-lb missile leaving the aeroplane is somewhat hard to miss – yet inside the cockpit on the armament status panel I had an indication telling me that all four missiles were still remaining. I knew what I'd felt, even though there were now conflicting cockpit cues, so I knew that it had come off.

AWACS was instrumental in very nearly every kill scored by the F-15 during *Desert Storm*. The crews of these irreplaceable assets were particularly challenged early on in the campaign, when it was expected that Iraq would scramble a sizeable counter-air force, swamping radar screens with intermingled returns from friendly and hostile fighters. But that never happened, and the IrAF response to the opening shots of the war was underwhelming, and, for the most part, AWACS performed its job with great success. (*USAF*)

'After I had shot my missile I started dropping chaff and flying defensive manoeuvres in case he had shot at me. I also wanted to get down low to cause him some look-down/shoot-down problems – it was time to get lower and manoeuvre away. In this case the chaff and manoeuvring broke his lock, and with the spike gone, I turned in and pointed at the contact once again. I then saw him blow up at co-altitude (and approximately ten miles away). It was nothing like the red glowing fireballs that you hear about – it was a bright purplish-white colour that lasted three to five seconds. Then it was dark again.'

The MiG-29 pilot went down with his jet and was killed. He is believed to have been Capt Omar Goben, who had previously flown MiG-21s and MiG-23s, and who had two IRIAF F-5 kills to his name.

During the engagement Kelk had manoeuvred defensively to the west, but Williams had manoeuvred to the east, separating them by some distance. To complicate matters, Tollini's reactions to his own spike had prompted him to also manoeuvre to the east, putting him on a potential collision course with Kelk to his right – recollections from Tollini and Kelk about who turned east and who turned west are conflicting. As if that was not enough, in the confusion that followed, Tollini locked up Williams and began the process of identifying him, uncertain of whether he was Kelk's original target! He was not sure of the ID and held his fire. Instead, Tollini made a night visual ID:

'"Willy" passed very close – directly underneath me – and I recognised the cockpit lighting of an F-15C.'

Williams had also flown a defensive manoeuvre because he had been spiked by the same MiG Kelk had just downed:

'But we stuck to the game plan and flew our assigned flow. I was a little concerned because I had ordered that external tanks be jettisoned after the engagement, but my jettison had failed and I was carrying this extra weight around that I did not want. I was trying to keep up and build up speed without using afterburner, and I was playing catch-up with Williams, trying to rejoin without giving away my position – afterburner is highly visible at night. We continued north towards Baghdad and, when I was no longer spiked, I performed a radar sanitisation and did not find anyone else in front of me.

'I eventually rejoined with Williams based on timings and pre-assigned headings and altitudes – I asked him to give me a quick flash of his beacons (lights) and I saw him about 1.5 miles ahead of me. We got to about 30 to 40 miles south of Baghdad and then commenced a left turn to the west to clear out the H1 and H2 airfields. We did not see anyone, so we flowed to the south and across the border again. I had one unnerving spike as we headed south-bound – it was at my "six o'clock" close, and lasted about five seconds before it went away. I never saw it again.'

Kelk's kill was verified the next morning by Intelligence as a MiG-29 'Fulcrum'. He was the first American to score a kill in the F-15.

With 'Pennzoil' flight approximately 100 miles ahead to the northeast, and committed to intercepting the two groups of 'bogeys' called out by AWACS, 'Citgo' flight pushed northwest towards Mudaysis AB – a small airfield used by forward-deployed IrAF assets, and with an alert component of Mirage F 1EQs.

Capt Robert 'Cheese' Graeter – the same pilot who had flown cover for US Navy P-3s during the KAL 007 incident some eight years prior – was leading the flight in F-15C 85-0105, call-sign 'Citgo 61':

'My number two was Lt Scott Maw, number three was Lt Col Bill Thiel and number four was Lt Robert Brooks. The initial push was totally screwed up. Mine was the first four-ship to hit the tanker, and getting gas was probably the scariest part of the whole mission. There were six KC-135s flying in the weather, and we had to find our tanker by coming in laterally without using the radio, maintaining 500 ft vertical separation, with no lights and using Mode 2 IFF. It took twice as long as usual to get our gas – it was very bumpy. We were in and out of weather and there was no moon.'

'Pennzoil' rolled up behind 'Citgo' and awaited its turn on the tanker. Tollini later told Graeter that he had been so spatially disorientated whilst following him and the KC-135 that he could have sworn on the Bible that that they were doing barrel rolls as they took on fuel. The conditions were so severe that Graeter checked the time, did some mental calculations, and then decided to take his flight south, out of the weather:

'My wingmen had been with me in the weather for the better part of an hour. I wanted them to take a breath and relax for a little, because the weather, formation, and tanking really was a handful. I sent them out to trail formation to let the radar work for them for a little while.'

Nearing the push time, he gathered them in closer once again:

'I'd done all of the timing calculations, so as we approached we began to leave our holding area to hit our push-point at 0310 hrs. AWACS started having concerns right on 0300 hrs, and called us to commit early, which is why we ended up in trail to "Pennzoil" flight. It takes almost 12 minutes to get to a stage where we can think about being tactical. As I led the flight above a cirrus cloud deck, we got some starlight, and I was working the radar trying to find "Pennzoil", which I eventually did.'

Interestingly, Graeter chose not to fly a 'wall' formation that evening. The relative merits of the formation – namely, its ability to bring maximum firepower and radar coverage to bear – were outweighed, in

IrAF MiG-29 29060 is seen taxiing out at a defence exhibition held in Baghdad in May 1989. Iraq was slow to introduce the type to service, even though it ordered over 130 examples from the former USSR. Although the first six MiG-29s were delivered to Iraq in 1987, by January 1991 only one unit – No 4 Sqn – was considered operational, and even then it lacked night-qualified pilots. The squadron was to be mauled badly in a series of skirmishes with USAF F-15Cs, and also suffered cases of fratricide. (*US DoD via Tom Cooper*)

his opinion, by the workload it induced on his wingmen. Maw and Brooks were young pilots who were new to the jet, while Thiel was experienced, but not a FWS graduate like Graeter, and Tollini, and Kelk in 'Pennzoil' flight. In summary, Graeter felt that the 'wall' was an additional burden that he did not want to place upon his flight. Instead, he chose a more orthodox night-time formation:

'Maw was to my right at about 40 degrees, while Lt Col Thiel was staggered back about 15 miles in an offset trail to my left, with Brooks to his left. The formation provided us with some nose-tail separation so that we could manoeuvre without worrying about bumping into one another.'

'Citgo' was tasked to run directly at Mudaysis, then to turn northwest towards H2 and H3. Once there, Graeter was to set up a Barrier CAP (BARCAP) of two 25-mile legs between H2/H3 and Mudaysis, with a pair of Eagles on each leg. This would allow them to commit against IrAF fighters ascending from either base:

'As we ran towards Mudaysis, I could see all of the F-15Es on Mode 4 (IFF). We could also see a CAP of MiG-29s 50 to 60 miles northwest of Mudaysis and about 85 miles from us, but they were all we could see. I was pretty confident that the MiG-29s I could see were the same ones that AWACS was talking about because I was not getting a Mode 4 response from them. We were closing the distance on them, but we were not running an intercept on them just yet.'

As 'Citgo' closed the gap, Graeter began to pick up new contacts over the top of Mudaysis:

'I got a contact at low altitude, which was my search area of responsibility. I had my radar set to search from ground level upwards to about 18 miles in front of me. Maw had the opposite area, and was looking from 50,000 ft downwards. At 25 miles, my first contact appeared to be at about 1500 ft AGL (Above Ground Level), on a departure heading northwest. He started a left-hand turn to the southeast, so I broke the lock and observed additional jets taking off. I could now see three contacts, all in a few miles trail.'

Maw and Graeter melded their radar images and sorted their targets (both Mirage F 1EQs) in order to execute a coordinated plan of attack. At 17 miles, Graeter locked up the lead target and Maw concentrated on the trailing jet:

'I still had no idea what type of threat they were, but AWACS was getting information from *Rivet Joint*, and was calling "pop-up threats", which meant that there were hostiles within 25 miles. I learned later from listening to the

A large strike force of F-15E Strike Eagles was under threat at the time the 58th TFS's Robert Graeter scored his second kill during the first night of the war. Whilst rueful at the death of the two Mirage pilots, he was under no misconceptions that his foe had taken off with the explicit intent of intercepting and downing the bomb-laden Strike Eagles. (*Gary Klett via Author*)

tapes that the AWACS controller was also referring to them as bandits, although I didn't know that at the time. I was therefore working through my NCTR and IFF EID "tree", manually dialling in my Mode 3 7600 to see if anyone was "squawking" a comm failure, but getting no return.

'In the meantime, I was having to ramp it downhill from 30,000 ft to the "mid 20s" because my radar look-angle was getting a bit steep. I finally finished my EID matrix at about ten miles or so, but I was still asking AWACS for confirmation of the status of this guy [Graeter never heard the original AWACS call confirming that the target was a bandit]. I got no response, so I went ahead and shot him from a distance of ten miles.'

In contrast to Kelk, Graeter watched his AIM-7 come off of the right side of the jet, despite telling himself that he wouldn't:

'Our game plan was to shoot and look to see if the rocket motor had fired, and to check that the missile was looking good to intercept. So that's what I did. I then got back into the cockpit and flew my F-pole manoeuvre, executing a 40-degree check turn to the left to give the missile and me some added space. By the time I looked back outside, I could no longer see the missile, and, as the computer told me that the weapon was about to time out, I started to pull my nose back towards the target. That's when the missile went off.

'I distinctly remember the missile exploding in a conical shape as the charge went off. Everything coming off of it was red hot, so it was easy for me to see this cone of energy. Instantaneously, some four or so miles from me, at a height of 7000 ft, debris started coming from the other direction – southeast – as the target exploded with a really bright flash. Pieces of the jet continued to arc earthwards in flames from the southeast. I called, "Splash", and Maw confirmed that he could see it.'

Maw was still locked onto the trailing Mirage F 1EQ, which was 15 miles ahead of him. The remaining two F-15s in 'Citgo' flight, which had fallen back into a 20-mile trail, had already been despatched to the northwest by Graeter after he directed them to H2 and H3. They were to cut-off any support that may have been launched in response to these initial engagements between the IrAF and the F-15Cs. Neither found anything of interest, so they executed a CAP over the original BARCAP coordinates instead. Capt Graeter recalled:

'I checked to the northwest, went to Auto Guns and slewed the radar down, looking for the downed Mirage's wingman. As I listened to Maw calling his bandit at 330 degrees for 13 miles, there was another explosion – the jet I had just shot had impacted the ground. Almost immediately afterwards, another aircraft hit the ground at my "two o'clock" about three miles away from where the first Mirage had come down. I could see the burning jet tumbling and cart-wheeling across the desert floor. There was an overcast, so the light from the explosions bounced off of the cloud deck – it was pretty surreal.

'As best as we could tell, the pilot of the number two Mirage had gone into a hard right turn to the west in an effort to get away from us, suffered spatial disorientation and then flown into the ground.'

By now the pilot of a third Mirage that had taken off from Mudaysis had a fairly good idea that he was outclassed, and in a perilous situation. The Iraqi quickly headed back north towards his base, putting Maw in a ten-mile tail-chase situation. Several factors combined to prevent Graeter, who was closer than Maw by several miles, from going after the fleeing Mirage – Roland surface-to-air missile (SAM) indications were coming from the vicinity of Mudaysis, and he was also detecting SAM activity in the H2/H3 airfield complex to the northwest. An excessive look-down radar angle was also required to detect the low-flying Mirage, and he did not want to light his afterburners to give chase in case he attracted attention to himself.

For the first time, the odds were stacked in the Mirage pilot's favour. Graeter told the author that to this day, he would have been hard-pressed to have got him, 'even with AMRAAM'.

'Citgo' flight learned from the wing's intelligence officer upon landing at Tabuk that their quarry had been Mirage F 1EQs. Graeter was officially awarded credit for the second Mirage as a 'manoeuvring kill' one week later. Suggestions that credit for this victory should have been attributed to an EF-111A, which allegedly out-manoeuvred the Mirage after being pursued by it, were dismissed as 'highly unlikely' by the MiG killers interviewed for this book by the author. Graeter himself recalled that there were no EF-111As in the area that night, the only Coalition aircraft nearby being F-15Es.

Upon landing back at Tabuk, Graeter's thoughts turned to the Iraqi pilot he had just killed:

'There was no chance of surviving a hit by a big missile like an AA-10 (which the IrAF used) or AIM-7. You were not going to bail out, you were not going to make a radio call – you were going to turn into dust. That AIM-7 warhead absolutely shredded the Mirage. It's designed to cut the cockpit into shreds when fired in a head-on engagement – the pilot never knew what hit him. When I got back, we debriefed with the intel people and then headed to the food hall for breakfast. Chuck Magill, who had just got up in preparation for his day flight, told me later that he could tell from my face that this was not all fun and games.'

Magill could not possibly have known it, but he too would be experiencing the same emotions as Graeter within hours.

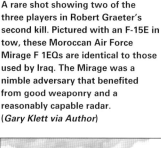

A rare shot showing two of the three players in Robert Graeter's second kill. Pictured with an F-15E in tow, these Moroccan Air Force Mirage F 1EQs are identical to those used by Iraq. The Mirage was a nimble adversary that benefited from good weaponry and a reasonably capable radar. (*Gary Klett via Author*)

'I looked like that because I was thinking, "I just killed a guy, and then I watched another die"', Graeter reflected. 'I am the kind of person who thought that the Iraqi pilot probably had a wife and family like me, and that he was just doing his job. It was hard.' Maw reminded Graeter that the Mirage pilots had taken off to kill the F-15Es, and that they would have done the same to him had they been given the chance.

'You never reconcile with the fact you have killed someone. Never. You just accept it and deal with it as best you can', Graeter concluded 12 years later.

As 'Citgo' and 'Pennzoil' flights conducted their sweeps in southwestern Iraq, Capt Steve 'Tater' Tate (flying F-15C 83-0017, call-sign 'Quaker 11') of the 71st TFS led four-ship package 'Quaker 11' to '14' on a sweep and CAP within the eastern zone in support of a mixed SEAD/strike package. The four F-15s separated into pairs, with 'Quaker 13' and '14' (Capts Damian Harp and Mark Atwell) flying a high CAP at 30,000 ft over Al Jawah AB, while 'Quaker 11' and '12' executed a low CAP at 10,000 ft to engage any aircraft detected flying along a known threat axis.

Despite an erroneous vector from AWACS to a bogey that turned out to be an F-111, Tate and his wingman, Capt Bo Merlack, were soon vectored onto another contact which was heading west, and appeared to be threatening a flight of F-4Gs. Tate later recalled:

'I finished my turn and then picked the contact up on radar about 16 miles off my nose (at 8000 ft). I was talking to AWACS about who this contact was, and what he was, but they did not have a good idea, so I started getting all of my (EID) systems to work. At about 12 miles in front of me, the target met the ROE to allow me to shoot at it. I buried my head in the radar tube to prevent any flash blindness, made sure that the target was definitely hostile and shot an AIM-7 Sparrow off of the right side.'

Tate then executed his 'F-pole' manoeuvre:

'As the missile went off, I checked away from it a little bit, called out "Fox 1 against a Mirage F 1", to AWACS and my wingman, and right about this time they started shooting SAMs at us.'

At this extremely early stage in the war the Iraqi IADS was fully operational, and the IrAF GCI system that controlled its fighters was also up and running.

Scoring the 1st TFW's only kill of the war elevated Steve Tate's standing within the wing, but it was American news network CNN which placed him in the world's spotlight, reporting – incorrectly – that he had scored the first kill of the war. This error, which some attribute to the clever alacrity of the 1st TFW public affairs team and the fortuitous placement of the CNN crew at the right moment, would take years to rectify (USAF)

F-15C 82-0009 was the aircraft assigned to 71st TFS Mirage F 1 killer Steve Tate, although he was flying 83-0017 when he claimed his victory on the first night of the war. This Eagle was photographed by RAF Tornado F 3 pilot Ian Black at Dhahran in late 1990. (Ian Black via the Author)

Two 71st TFS F-15Cs sit side-by-side in a revetment at Dhahran during *Desert Shield*, their canopies cranked open to avoid excessive heat build up in the cockpits. Neither jet boasts any external armament. (*Ian Black via the Author*)

However, over the next few days it was repeatedly attacked and dismembered, but in those early hours of the war SAM batteries resisted firing at Coalition aircraft when there was a possibility that they might hit one of their own jets.

'I started to get spiked by an I-HAWK, which was a US-built SAM system that the Iraqis stole from Kuwait when they invaded, so I was very nervous about that. I looked out to my left towards Baghdad and saw some SAMs coming up, but on both sides, wherever I looked, there was AAA (anti-aircraft artillery).

'With about two or three seconds of flying time left on my AIM-7 before it impacted the Mirage, I started to turn back towards the target. The missile looked good to me, so I elected not to fire another weapon – if it had missed him for some reason then I could have followed up with another shot, but he was not manoeuvring, so I felt it was looking good. The jet blew up and I flew a big turn away from it, the sky really lighting up for a second. I could see it disintegrating, with big parts splitting off and then breaking up into smaller pieces as this huge streamer of burning metal fell to the ground.'

Tate's kill was the only one scored by the 1st TFW during the war.

On what was the 33rd TFW's first daylight mission of the war, US Marine Corps Capt Chuck 'Sly' Magill, who was on an exchange tour with the USAF, led 'Zerex', 'Pennzoil' and 'Union' F-15 flights in protection of a strike force of 50 other Coalition aircraft on 17 January. The 58th TFS's 'Zerex' flight (Magill's four-ship) consisted of Lt Mark Arriola in the number two jet, Capt Rhory 'Hoser' Draeger in the third machine and Capt Tony 'Kimo' Schiavi in the fourth F-15. 'Pennzoil' flight, led by Tollini, also came from the 58th TFS, leaving Langley's 71st TFS to provide the eight jets of 'Union' flight.

In total, some 16 F-15Cs would be responsible for protecting an entire strike package of 40 F-16s, eight F-4Gs and two EF-111s. The F-16s' targets consisted of the airfields at Al Taqaddum and Al Assad, and specifically a biological and chemical warfare research building located within the perimeter of Al Taqaddum.

The 58th TFS four-ships took off at 1400 hrs local, rendezvoused with the tanker and then pushed north into Iraq. AWACS initially had problems getting onto the frequency-hopping 'Have Quick' radio

Chuck Magill, seen here (right) with Tony Schiavi, was a Marine Corps captain who had transferred from F/A-18 Hornets to fly Eagles in a three-year exchange tour with the US Air Force. He proved to be calm and collected in the heat of battle, and was much admired by those who flew with him. He remains active in the fighter community today, and lectures on fighter tactics at the US Navy's Topgun fighter weapons school at NAS Fallon, Nevada, when not keeping his hand in flying with the USMC Reserve. (*Tony Schiavi via Author*)

network, but this was eventually resolved, much to the relief of the F-15 pilots. Capt Magill recalled:

'I had my eight Eglin Eagles in close so that we could provide a pre-strike BVR sweep of the target area. These airfields had not been touched so far, so the overall mission commander in the lead F-16 had already decided that if we ran into too much opposition the mission would be scrubbed.'

Some 50 to 70 Mirage F 1s, MiG-23s and MiG-25s were believed to be based at Al Taqaddum, while the IrAF's MiG-29 force was amongst the 50 fighters based at Al Assad.

Crossing the border, Magill (flying F-15C 85-0107, call-sign 'Zerex 71') placed his eight-ship sweep flight some 80 miles ahead of the main strike force. Pushing from the 30°N 42°E holding point, he was advised by AWACS over secure radio that it had two bandits southwest of the target area at medium altitude:

'AWACS gave us clearance to fire on these guys, which was remarkable given that they were about 160 miles away. The bandits were flying a north-south BARCAP south of Taqaddum AB, but I was not worried about them at this point. I was going to continue my game plan, which was to sweep the entire area in a counter-clockwise flow – Al Taqaddum, Al Assad, and then on over to H2/H3, before leaving the country.

'I had my four-ship on my left, "Pennzoil 5" to "8" off to my right, abreast with me, and I was thinking more about the number of bandits, rather than what they were actually doing over there. The fact that AWACS had called two bandits was making me think that there would be closer to 20 by the time we actually got there! I was thinking that the MiGCAP was probably more of an airborne radar system to make up for the fact that we had taken out a lot of their long-range radars the night before.'

If faced with overwhelming numbers, Magill planned to execute long-range AIM-7 shots before disengaging to the south under the cover of the Langley F-15s, which were positioned directly above the main strike force some 13 minutes' flying time away.

'I did not want to fly directly over Mudaysis AB, where Rob Graeter had scored his kills six hours earlier, so we bypassed it to the east by 40 to 50 miles. As we pressed towards the MiGs, closing to 40 miles, I could see that they were slow and low, on a maximum endurance profile in a "Gomer" echelon formation. They were flying at a speed of about 360 knots at 1500 ft, and the trailer was just swinging left and right behind his lead. As we painted them (with the radar), all we could see was two targets, so I now knew that we didn't need eight Eagles to take these guys on. I duly sent Rick Tollini and his four-ship off to the northwest up towards Al Assad so that they could make sure that nothing hopped out of there.'

As Tollini checked northwest, Magill's flight overflew a large Iraqi armoured battalion, which engaged them with various SAMs:

'The missiles were targeted in what we call an uncorrelated fashion. That is to say that they were locked on, but we couldn't tell on who. Therefore, we all broke at the same time. I was on the right-hand side, with my number two east of me, and Rhory Draeger and Tony Schiavi were on my left. I called "Combat 1", which was the order to jettison our wing tanks, and we dumped chaff and flares as we manoeuvred. In a remarkable bit of flying, we evaded these missiles, and dropped from 30,000 ft to 18,000 ft in the process. As I came out of my aggressive break, having lost 12,000 ft, and with the noise of the radios, engines and RWR gear going off, there on my right was my wingman, still holding his position.'

Hard-crewing in the build up to *Desert Storm* had once again worked for the 'Gorillas', enabling a very talented Lt Arriola to maintain two-ship integrity with his leader in the most demanding of conditions. Magill continues:

'We were now heading east, and so too were "Hoser" and "Kimo". As we cleared the threat, and pitched back towards Al Taqaddum, I looked left, and there were my Nos 3 and 4 in perfect position five miles west and slightly below me, so we immediately got back to our BRA (Bearing, Range, Altitude) reports on the MiGs.'

The missile launches had severely disrupted the flow of the engagement, coming as it did at the range – 40 miles – at which Magill had hoped to have the MiGs firmly sorted and tracked by:

'It was a shock to not know that something was there in the first place, but more so because it came at the time when I was thinking about engaging what we believed then to be a very capable fighter.

'We regrouped and tightened up our wall formation, but my attitude was now changed, and my blood was boiling. The SAM launches had really made me angry, and it was then that I realised that this was really happening – there would be no "knock it off!" call today. We got to about 32 miles from the MiGs when they turned back "cold" ["hot" and "cold" are terms used to describe a target's aspect relative to the launch aircraft – "hot" targets flying towards it and "cold" targets fly away.] As soon as they did that, I called, "Push it up! Push it up!", and all four of us went into full AB and ramped it downhill to go as fast as the sucker could take us. I was thinking that the MiGs would either land and the whole fleet would then launch at us, or that they would land and that would be the end of the story.'

But Magill was wrong on both counts. As he closed the range to 26 miles, the MiGs reacted, turning lazily back to the south, while simultaneously accelerating from 360 to 560 knots – fighting speed.

'We were doing about 600 knots, so we now had 1200 knots of closure! What had been happening slowly was now happening very fast, and by the time we got to a 20-mile separation, they were totally "hot", just finishing their turn to a bearing of 240 degrees. We were on a 30-degree bearing when Draeger fired first and crossed over my nose above me, telling me that he'd shot the guy on my side. We usually used an azimuth sort, but the No 2 MiG has tucked in really close to his lead, and it took a couple of sweeps of my radar before I could target him and fire.'

Because of the proximity of the two 'Fulcrums', Draeger had engaged the eastern MiG rather than the western one, forcing him to cut over the top of Magill as he executed his F-pole. Consequently, Magill had to positively acquire the western MiG before he engaged,

lest he shoot his No 3 down in error. The contact breakout was eventually forthcoming, and Magill wasted no time in firing.

'My first (AIM-7) missile looked like it did not have a good flight profile – it headed straight for the deck. I offset (F-pole) to the right to slow down the engagement, but I didn't like the way the missile was flying so I came back, centred the dot, then fired the second (AIM-7) missile. As it came off, time stopped. I remember vividly the missile's brown and yellow bands, and the way that it rolled as it flew out in front of me. I then offset once again.

'We got a visual on the MiGs, still in the same formation, at about seven miles. No 3's missile hit his MiG square in the canopy, and that was the end of the story for that one. My first missile came up from below, hitting the other MiG in the right wing root and tearing a good piece of that wing off. As he nosed down, my second missile went right through the middle of his fuselage. It looked like a "T-bone".'

Magill and Draeger called their kills in, and they were surprised to hear the radio come alive with cheers of support and appreciation from the strikers.

'It was a surprise because our comm had been impeccable up until that point. I maintained focus though – when you fly the F-15 in a multi-bogey environment, it is highly visible. You can ask anyone and they'll agree. We blew through the merge, kept the speed on and used our radars in case there were any trailers, but the four of us were clean.'

In the post-merge, Magill looked at his fuel state and identified that he did not have enough 'gas' to fly the remainder of the planned flow to Al Assad and H2/H3. He also became cognisant of the fact that there was increasingly more green vegetation below him, signifying that he was getting closer to the Euphrates River, and therefore too close to the target. He converted his airspeed into altitude and called for an in-place Immelman turn to rapidly place them at 25,000 ft.

'It was a good idea to gain the altitude, but a bad idea overall because it placed us right in the middle of a SAM engagement zone. Immediately, as I was upside down and heading south, I got multiple SAM and launch warnings (SA-2 and SA-3). I looked at the RWR and saw that the range was perfect for the SAMs, so I peered out of my canopy and rolled wings level. Then I saw the missiles, like little space shuttles with booster phases that let them climb up over the top of me, before arching back down, straight at me.

'It was laughable, because I was telling everyone that I was being targeted, and I then heard, "Two's clean", "Three's clean" and "Four's

Firing the AIM-7 at night left little room for doubt in the pilot's mind that the missile had left the jet, but during the day it was a different story. Pumped with adrenaline and focused on a myriad of attention getters – threat, wingman, RWR etc. – it was easy for the pilot to be unsure as to whether the missile had indeed been released. Add to the equation unusual flight attitudes, the fact that many pilots had never fired a live Sparrow before and that nearly all the MiG killers interviewed for this book suffered from considerable temporal distortion, and clearly there existed some margin for confusion. (Gary Klett via Author)

clean", in response. I was the only guy being targeted! I punched off my centreline fuel tank and broke left and right to get away from the threat, then my fuel gauge went to zero. The missiles were relatively easy to defeat, although I lost about 15,000 ft in the process of doing so.'

Egressing the area, Magill offset to the west by some 60 degrees to steer clear of the ingressing strike force (which he worried might mistake him for an Iraqi fighter and engage him), and then conducted a battle-damage check to establish whether his faulty fuel gauge had been caused by SAM or AAA debris. There was none, and 'Zerex' flight landed back at Tabuk without further incident. The fuel gauge fault was later traced to a faulty 'pig-tail' wire on the centreline pylon.

Whilst this mission would make the history books as the first daylight raid of *Desert Storm*, it should also be recognised as a missed opportunity for the IrAF to have made a stand following its beating at the hands of the USAF

SAM sites such as these posed a near-constant threat to marauding Eagle pilots intent on both protecting their strike-fighter brethren and prosecuting any Iraqi pilot who ventured into the air. It took enormous presence of mind and task prioritisation to remain fully aware of the location and reach of these SAMs, especially when intercepts – which in themselves could cause cognitive saturation – reached their climax.
(*Gary Klett via Author*)

F-15s the previous night. With many of the SAM systems overlooking the target area not due for attack by Coalition forces until later in the war, and therefore operating with relative impunity, and with both Al Taqaddum and Al Assad bristling with fighters, the outcome of this mission could have easily been different.

Following the initial wave of attacks in the early hours of 17 January, the IrAF had reacted just as expected – launching alert fighters and vectoring CAP fighters towards groups of Coalition strikers. These threat aircraft had quickly been neutralised, forcing the Iraqis to consolidate on Day 2. By Day 3 the IrAF was once again ready to mount operations. It was about to lose another seven fighters to the F-15 force in a single 24-hour period.

At Tabuk AB on 19 January, it was Capt Richard 'Kluso' Tollini's turn to lead a mission in support of F-15Es searching for elusive mobile Scud launchers. His four-ship OCA flight, call-sign 'Citgo', remained unchanged from the first mission, and he launched (in F-15C 85-0101) at 1630 hrs with Pitts (in F-15C 85-0099), Kelk and Williams in tow.

The 58th TFS's Weapons Officer, Tollini had been christened 'Kluso' on account of his physical similarity to the Peter Sellers character *Inspector Clouseau* Tollini's antagonist, and old friend, 'Budge' Wilson had coined the call-sign, but chosen the phonetic spelling because it would be easier for other fighter pilots to get right!

He had been woken at midnight some four months before the start of the war by his wing commander, who gave him 30 minutes to pack his bags and get out to the ramp to meet a Learjet that would whisk him off to Riyadh. Tollini had been assigned the role of 33rd TFW mission planner, and was briefed on the highly classified plans for the opening stages of the war. He returned to Tabuk, forbidden from sharing the planning workload with fellow pilots despite his protestations that the task was too time-consuming for a single person,

Sitting in the relative safety of the revetments at Dhahran, two 71st TFS jets await their next mission. Assigned to the 1st TFW since its delivery to the USAF on 1 July 1984, the Eagle in the foreground (83-0010) was deployed with the wing's 94th FS to Incirlik, in Turkey, as part of Operation *Northern Watch* on the eve of Operation *Iraqi Freedom* in 2003. (*Ian Black via Author*)

Tollini duly conducted framework planning of the missions that the ATO called for the 58th TFS to execute. He also worked with a similarly appointed representative from the 1st TFW – Maj Denny Krimble – to share out ATO tasking requests, and ensure that the F-15C would meet the expectations of those at the top of the chain of command. When it became clear that war was imminent, 'Kluso' was given permission to brief his flight leads and weapons instructors on the plans – this took place a week before the start of *Desert Storm*.

Larry Pitts was a recently upgraded two-ship flight lead with 300 hours in the F-15. Along with the likes of Magill, Graeter and Draeger, he was amongst the first to be cleared to hear the details of the ATO from Tollini around Christmas time 1990. He assisted by visiting the aircraft carrier USS *Saratoga* (CV-60) whilst Tollini journeyed out to USS *John F Kennedy* (CV-67) in an effort to establish deconfliction, ROE, and mission coordination with their US Navy counterparts.

The two men had been through Officer Training School, Undergraduate Pilot training, *Red Flag,* and now Operation *Desert Shield* together, and were (and remain) the best of friends. They flew together on many a six-hour HVA CAP sortie before the war, sandwiching themselves in between Iraqi fighters conducting routine training missions across the border and the AWACS or tanker they were assigned to protect. Afterwards, they would hypothesise over cigarettes and coffee that when they finally got to engage the IrAF, they might actually end up pitting their skills not against Iraqis, but against Russian advisors known to be in-country training local pilots.

The bond between Tollini and Pitts was certainly not unique – the USAF fostered and encouraged such camaraderie – but it *was* significant because, in the heat of the engagement that followed, it cemented the training, tactics, and doctrine that had been instilled in them from the start of their careers as Eagle pilots.

Larry Pitts remembers:

'By Day 3 we had realised that the IrAF was not going to pose as great a threat as we thought it would. We flew two missions that day, the first of which was cancelled due to weather – but it still required us to stay on the tanker for six hours because there was intelligence that Saddam Hussein was going to try and leave the country, and senior commanders wanted us to shoot that flight down. Having hung on to the tanker for six hours, we went back thinking that we were going to have the day off.

'As soon as we landed, the Ops Officer told us to get gas and take off again, so we refuelled, got airborne and then rendezvoused with a tanker south of the border. AWACS called two groups of enemy fighters 60 miles north of us just as we were coming off the tanker.'

The flight pushed north at 25,000 ft to engage the first group, which was dead ahead and 15,000 ft below.

'As we pressed closer, another group appeared about 30 degrees to the right of us and about 60 miles out – both groups were closing on us', Pitts added.

Tollini recalled that AWACS had erroneously identified both groups as MiG-29s, but he was more concerned with the fighters' intentions:

'It looked to me like they were doing some kind of a decoy tactic to get us to go after one while the other came in behind us. We got into a cut-off intercept on the first group from the south west, pointing towards Baghdad, while they were headed due south from Al Assad or Al Taqaddum airfield, northwest of Baghdad. At 35 miles we locked them up and they started heading east towards Baghdad. As we chased them, we saw the second group in a 30-mile lead-trail formation with the first group, flying in a north-south orientation. That's what made it look like a decoy tactic to me.'

Tollini continued to monitor the first group as it headed off to the northeast, then checked his flight to the north to go head on with the second group as it came south:

'Once we locked the second group up they also manoeuvred – this time to the west – and I remember that as they turned through west to the north, I thought we were going to have to chase them. Fairly quickly they did a 270-degree turn to the south, coming straight at us from 30 miles out in a three- or five-mile lead-trail formation, down around 3000 ft MSL (Mean Sea Level – about 2000 ft Above Ground Level). My intention was to shoot a couple of AIM-7s and kill these guys BVR, so I locked the lead and "J B" Kelk locked the trailer.'

With their concentration now focused exclusively on the south-bound MiGs in front of them, Pitts recalled that the target jets executed a defensive manoeuvre:

'"Kluso" got a good lock, and was ready to shoot at targeting range, when the MiGs went to the beam [perpendicular to Tollini and Pitts] and took it down low. We lost them, "Kluso" never got his missile off and we totally lost SA for a little bit. As we kept pushing north, we realised that one guy had come back in "hot". He was coming left-to-right across our formation, five miles in front of us, at 300 ft and doing 700 knots. He had also lost his SA, and didn't know that we were there.'

Larry Pitts' engagement with a 'Foxbat' on 19 January was one of the few aerial actions in *Desert Storm* that was both testing *and* protracted. Pitts remained with the USAF after the war, and recently became the Commandant of the USAF's Officer Training School. (*Larry Pitts via Author*)

Being on the extreme left side of the F-15s' wall formation, Mark Williams was the first to see the MIG-25 'Foxbat' as it crossed from left to right in front of the 58th TFS pilots. However, it was Pitts who was in the best position to engage:

'I called "Engaged!" and locked him up with my radar in a high-to-low weapons conversion, where I actually pulled 12G [the F-15's maximum allowable is 9G] and seriously over-stressed the jet! He was going so fast, however, that as soon as I locked him up he "gimballed" [flew off the radar's coverage] me, and I began to think that I would never find him again because he was going like stink.

'This was the second mission of the day, the weather was bad and he was now on top of a low overcast, and as I did the conversion, I saw him again and re-locked him with Auto Acq. As soon as I did that, he went into a defensive turn and broke into me, going from an easterly heading through south and then back to west. By the time he turned from west to north, I was in weapons parameters and at a fighting speed of about 420–450 knots, but he was way above the Mach, flying this huge defensive turn.

'I easily got inside his turn and again called "Engaged!" because I had not heard "Kluso" clear me to fire. "Kluso" responded with "Press!", which made me flight lead for a short time, and indicated that he was now supporting me.

'I was now 9000 ft feet behind the guy, and close to a tail aspect, so I selected an AIM-9. I got a good tone (the missile saw the target) and uncaged the weapon, after which I still had a good tone [the missile was tracking the target without the aid of the radar], so I launched. He immediately decoyed the AIM-9 with flares.'

The MiG's timely release of countermeasures had spoofed the missile into shifting track from its hot exhausts to the even hotter burning magnesium flare.

'As soon as he hit north, he stopped turning and tried to run, still at 300 ft and now doing 500 knots. I selected an AIM-7, felt the clunk as it released and then looked to the right and saw that it was almost flying in formation with me! The rocket motor then lit and it accelerated off right at him, and past his canopy without fusing.'

Now at 6000 ft, and with a pure tail aspect, Pitts re-selected the AIM-9, got a good tone, and uncaged:

'Just as I was about to fire, he put out more flares, dragging the missile's seeker head off before I could take the shot. I re-caged the weapon back to the radar, got a good tone and shot, but he again decoyed it with flares. He was fighting pretty hard, and I was thinking, "Man, I am going to have to gun this guy". I selected another AIM-7 and shot it, and this time the missile went right up my adversary's tailpipe and exploded. "Kluso" must have been thinking "'Cherry' needs some help here" at the same time, because he shot an AIM-9 which went straight into the fireball. The pilot bailed out and his ejection seat passed right over my canopy – I thought it was going to hit me – and I started hearing his emergency locator on GUARD [radio frequency].'

Pitts made his 'Splash' call and pulled up into a left-hand, climbing turn. As he did so, he saw the other 'Foxbat', and called, 'Two, second

MiG-25, my nose, five miles'. Tollini responded with, 'Engaged!', but struggled to immediately identify the jet as a MiG-25, F-15, or F-14.

Tollini recalled the engagement from his own perspective:

'I had "Willie" Williams searching high and "Cherry" Pitts searching low after the second group of MiGs beamed us and we lost them on radar. Fortunately, "Cherry" was able to grab the trailer as he finished his beam to the east and then turned due south again, and I actually got the lead jet back on radar momentarily before both of them flew off of our scopes. "Cherry's" guy started his right-hand turn underneath us, and my guy did a high-speed turn through the south, and I saw him leave the flight.'

Tollini transitioned from lead to wingman when Pitts called 'Engaged' on the first 'Foxbat'. He followed Pitts through the split-s manoeuvre that placed him behind the MiG-25:

'The MiG was in a right-hand turn and we were at very close range when "Cherry" camped behind him. I joined the fight in a left-hand turn from the southeast and cut across the circle as the MiG continued its turn from the west towards the northeast. It was then that "Cherry" started shooting off all of his missiles. He was not having any luck, so I radioed, "Two, come off", about which he later said to me, "'Kluso', I don't remember you saying that". My first shot got there a split-second later than his, and although I did not personally see the guy punch out, "Cherry" said that my missile got there seconds after the seat came out of the aircraft.'

With the troublesome 'Foxbat' dealt with, Tollini began his own engagement:

'As "Cherry" peeled off to the west, I flew right behind his MiG and watched it enter the undercast and impact the ground. We had already dropped our wing tanks, and we were all going really fast, so I pulled into a high-G right-hand turn through east to south. As I did that, I had an Auto Acq mode slewed out to the south – I think more by accident than planning – and as I came around the corner to the south, the radar grabbed the other guy as he came back into the fight.'

The 'Foxbat' re-entered the fight from a northerly heading, and although both Pitts and Tollini missed it at the time, AWACS had made a timely call to advise 'Citgo' flight of the impending merge. Tollini continued:

'The instant I snagged him, "Cherry" saw him visually and called him to me. Then it became an issue of ID again. When we merged the first time we had good ID, but having been spat out of the fight I didn't know who he was when he came back in again. I didn't know where "J B" and "Willie" had gone [they had actually departed the area to provide cover in case the original MiG-29 group attempted to pincer the flight], and I knew that there was a Navy package out there. This left me sitting barely a mile behind my target, looking at its tail, but unsure of what it was.

'What I *could* see was the jet's two huge burner plumes, so I asked on the radio if anyone was in burner. Having received various responses, I called everyone to get out of burner – working on the basis that if my target was indeed one of us its pilot would comply. Well, he didn't, so I looked at him more closely and saw that he had two missile

The huge twin afterburners of the MiG-25 'Foxbat' should have given Larry Pitts' AIM-9s a juicy target, but clever and persistent use of decoy flares and defensive manoeuvring forced him to work hard for his kill.
(*Mikoyan Gurevich Design Bureau*)

pylons under each wing. Now I knew that it was not an F-15 or F-14. That was the moment I *knew* that my target was a "Foxbat". Then I started shooting.'

The spare mental capacity that allowed Tollini to indulge in such dynamic thinking is a great indicator of how effective the USAF's F-15 pilot training has been over the years. At a time when temporal distortion, 'channelized' attention, fear and cognitive saturation can blunt the senses of any fighter pilot, Tollini's efforts to ID the target were characterised as 'outstanding' by Pitts.

With the MiG positively identified, Tollini closed for the kill:

'I was in full burner, camped back there in pure pursuit. The pilot of this aircraft was not like the first MiG in that he was not putting out any chaff or flares. Maybe he could not see me because I was camped in his "deep six", or maybe he'd run out of flares – I don't know. But he stayed in this high-G turn. My first AIM-7 was at low aspect, maybe 20 to 30 degrees off of the tail, and I hit the pickle button and waited, but I didn't see the missile flying out in front of me. We don't know for sure, but we think the rocket motor failed to light [the AIM-7 was less than reliable throughout the war, and Bitburg pilots in particular experienced a large number of malfunctions].

'I thumbed forward on the throttle-mounted weapons select switch to select an AIM-9, at which point what looked like a single flare popped out of the aircraft – it was not very bright, and it could have even been the pilot punching out, but I think I would have seen more flames if he had indeed ejected.

'In any case, I was not that confident that the AIM-9 would get there, having seen what happened to "Cherry's" missiles, so as soon as

I shot it I thumbed back to AIM-7 again. The AIM-9 flew close to his burner cans – through the plume – but then sailed wide and missed. I then shot the second AIM-7.'

In the temporal distortion that many pilots experienced at the time of their kills, Tollini watched the missile guide in a lag-pursuit mode for what seemed to him like minutes. It flew up from beneath the 'Foxbat' and then punctured its belly, exploding milliseconds later:

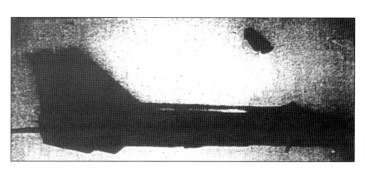

'The explosion was huge, like the Death Star from the *Star Wars* film! The "Foxbat" totally disintegrated, and I was amazed because that had not happened to "Cherry's" MiG.'

DEBRIEF

Despite the fact that Pitts had flown the visual engagement extremely well, and had employed his weapons properly, the first 'Foxbat' still required a total of five missiles to down it. To illustrate the point, every one of Pitts' shots would have been classed as kills in a peacetime exercise. He credits the 'Foxbat' pilot with having put up a good fight – one of the few IrAF pilots to do so throughout the war.

Tollini's main concern had been to end the fight as quickly as possible, and that remained the priority. AWACS was warning that the original group of IrAF fighters initially intercepted by the F-15s was now headed south again, and his flight had already been sucked into one merged engagement in what had been a fairly 'ugly' intercept. Fortunately Pitts and Tollini exited the area without any additional complications. The original group called out by AWACS failed to threaten either 'Citgo' flight or the strikers, although Kelk and Williams were still up high covering if they had.

The debrief for this flight was lengthy and intense. The mission had hardly gone according to plan, and there was no shying away from the customarily candid mission debrief – a *modus operandi* of everyday peacetime training that, 'Kluso' argues, is one of the reasons why the USAF was so successful in its quest to kill MiGs.

Did Pitts' and Tollini's hypothesis about Russian or ex-Soviet Bloc pilots come true? We will never know for sure, but Tollini offers this:

'Look at it this way. They were either the best or luckiest Iraqi pilots in the world, or they were not Iraqis at all. They should not have survived to the merge – our tactics, weapons and training should have seen to that – but these guys used tactics both before the merge and at the merge that really impressed me. I often wonder.'

As we shall see, there are others whose engagements have led them to believe much the same thing.

MORE KILLS FOR THE 58th

The 58th TFS claimed its eighth and ninth victories on 19 January, when Craig Underhill and Cesar Rodriguez received an airborne re-tasking at 1000 hrs local, some four hours into a six-hour E-3 and

This poor photograph is interesting because of the story behind it. Taken in late January 1991 by the crew of an Islamic Republic of Iran Air Force (IRIAF) F-4E Phantom II, it shows the pilot of an IrAF MiG-25PU ejecting from his aircraft inside Iranian airspace. The aircraft had previously been pursued by two USAF F-15Cs, which, apparently, fired several missiles at the fleeing 'Foxbat'. The Iraqi pilot engaged afterburners and escaped across the Iranian border. With his fuel finally depleted, and having been intercepted by the two IRIAF F-4Es, the pilot ejected. This "kill" was not credited to either the USAF or the IRIAF pilots.
(*Tom Cooper Collection via Author*)

KC-10 HVA CAP mission in the western sector. The mission leader, Capt (now Col) Cesar 'Rico' Rodriguez (flying F-15C 85-0114) described the events that followed as 'Iraq's ultimate attempt to score an airpower victory'.

The re-tasking came when Langley F-15s, which were supposed to provide a post-strike sweep, were unable to take-off. Rodriguez remembered:

'We were re-rolled to provide protection for a strike package – 36 to 38 F-16s and F-4Gs – that had not been on the ATO. As the tasking came through, we were approaching a refuelling decision, so I sent Nos 3 and 4 back to the tanker first and they then relieved us. As we were on our way to the tanker, we received the latest briefing from "Kluso", who was leading a four-ship ahead of us.'

Tollini was leading another 'Citgo' flight in support of the Scud-hunting F-15Es (see the action related previously in this chapter), but acted as a radio relay when the tasking came through.

Rodriguez received the strike's grid coordinates, special instructions and information associated with his mission. He then left the tanker and instructed Nos 3 and 4 to remain on the HVA CAP:

'I knew that by going as a two-ship, and with the first strikers on their way to the tanker by the time we got there, we'd have an increased risk factor – there was a fine balance between accepted risk and mission execution.

'The original plan called for the post-strike sweepers to fly behind the strikers, so we were prepared to be the "clean-up" guys. As it turned out, "Kluso's" flight was engaged in the same area as our strikers were heading, so we re-rolled once again to change from a post-strike sweep to a pre-strike sweep. That meant that we had to catch up and get ahead of our strikers so that we were in position to provide them with protection. We pushed it up and got high and fast, initially picking up a single contact to the northeast of the target area.'

As Rodriguez continued to speed towards the front of the package, he handed this contact off to Capt Craig 'Mole' Underhill (in F-15C 85-0122) to keep an eye on whilst he went back to search mode and found a group to the northwest of the target area:

'The biggest threat to the package was the northeastern contact, so I passed the northwestern group to AWACS in the hope that they would target them with a two-ship of OCA F-14s that were in the area. We put both radars into the eastern contact and flew a "vanilla intercept" – single contact breaks out into a group of two. We now knew that it was going to be a two-versus-two engagement, and that our opponents were MiG-29s, so we executed the press.

'The Iraqi pilots flew some anti-western manoeuvres to deny the radar accurate data and defeat the AIM-7. Prior to this mission, we had received intelligence that there would be pilots other than Iraqis participating in the air picture, and this validated, in my opinion, that possibility. These guys had it together, and knew what they had to do.'

The MiGs had beamed to the west, held the beam manoeuvre until out of the AIM-7 weapon engagement zone (WEZ) and then dragged 'Citgo 11' and '12' into the Baghdad 'Super MEZ' – the expansive missile engagement zone (MEZ) that covered Iraq's capital. The

Despite the extraordinary proceedings going on during *Desert Storm*, there remained the need for the usual administrative humdrum of squadron life to continue. Here, an F-15C pilot from the 1st TFW prepares to launch on his first CAP of the day. (*Ian Black via Author*)

manoeuvre did not fool Rodriguez, but it was clearly exceptionally well executed. Aware of the MiGs' intentions, he elected to continue the pursuit because he knew that it would allow the strikers to place bombs on target without harassment:

'We started to receive RWR indications that the SAMs were looking at us and getting ready to target us – we were also being informed that the last set of strikers were coming off target.'

Rodriguez turned his flight southwest just as the western AWACS informed him that there were bandits off of his right wing at 13 miles. The mission had been complicated by the need to transition from the western E-3 command and control structure to the central command and control structure following re-tasking to the post-strike sweep, and it quickly became clear that communications had broken down. This group was actually the same one that Rodriguez had handed off to the central AWACS controller to vector the Navy F-14s onto at the start of the push towards Baghdad:

'The central controller was having a hard time just keeping his area of responsibility (AOR) under control, so the western AWACS called on GUARD, "Pop-up contacts, 330 degrees for 13 miles". At 13 miles, I had no option but to disengage without any SA, so I directed an in-place turn to 330 degrees, jettisoned wing tanks and put my radar into the location of the target. I locked onto a target at eight miles and initiated my ID matrix, at which point I had an RWR indication that I had a "Slot Back" radar (MiG-29) locked onto me. I notched to the south and passed as much information to "Mole" as I could – "Altitude 8000 ft, off of my nose". My concern was self-preservation. I had 580 knots on the jet, I was well below 5000 ft and I was trying to stay on the beam while my ECM and chaff did all that they could.'

'Mole' locked the bandit up and used his own on-board systems and a call to an RC-135 *Rivet Joint* aircraft to secure positive confirmation that the target was indeed a MiG-29. Although at the time neither 'Rico' or 'Mole' knew it, a second 'Fulcrum' was some 12 miles behind its leader. Streaking south, Rodriguez looked over his right shoulder to see if he could spot the MiG:

'"Mole" fired a single AIM-7, and as he called "Fox 1", I looked over my left shoulder and saw his missile come off and fly out over the top of my tails. As the missile motor burned out, I looked to the left of the last source of smoke, at which point I picked up the silhouette of a MiG-29 roughly four miles off of my right wing. Shortly after that the missile impacted and there was nothing left – it's one of the embedded memories in my brain. There was the silhouette, and then seconds later there was literally nothing.'

For the duration of the engagement the MiG pilot had sustained a lock on 'Rico', but had been unable to employ his weapons. Rodriguez reckons that it was probably a combination of his ECM, chaff, and the efforts of other airborne platforms that denied the 'Fulcrum' pilot the ability to launch a missile at him.

'We then received another call from the western AWACS. "Second group, north, ten miles", at which point we executed an in-place check turn to the north. "Mole" and I were about 2.5-miles apart, and I was visual with him off my right wing, and slightly ahead. I looked up and saw a smoke trail – not a missile trail, but engine smoke – so I put my Auto Acq out there and "Mole" and I simultaneously locked him up.'

Underhill later wrote that the MiG initiated a hard turn into him when his Auto Acq mode triggered its RWR. Rodriguez continued:

'We started going through our ID matrix, and the target displayed a friendly electronic return to both of us. I directed a break lock and re-lock, but the same thing happened again. I now directed a VID pass, and pushed "Mole" out to a five-mile line-abreast formation. The bogey was closest in azimuth to my nose, so I flew the pass. I brought the Target Detection box [a square symbol in the HUD that is overlaid onto the radar-designated target's position] into view and looked at the contact at about eight miles, but it was just a dot and I couldn't tell what it was.

'I looked again at about four miles and saw a western-looking silhouette that resembled an F-15 or an F/A-18, so I don't declare him hostile. At about two miles I looked once again, but I was no longer thinking about taking a pre-merge shot, so I planned to merge with the bogey at 50 ft off of his left wing. As I crossed his wing-line, I saw that he was a brown- and green-camouflaged Iraqi MiG-29!'

The MiG was flying in the region of 8000 ft, and Rodriguez had flown a low-to-hi VID engagement *into* the sun, constantly staying below his adversary's plane of motion.

'I declared, "Hostile, MiG-29", and began a hard left turn when he started his left turn, so that we had what looked like a classic two-circle flight. Initially, his turn was level, so rather than stay horizontal with him I transitioned into a split-S manoeuvre to cut across his circle [turn]. "Mole" was now in the high 20,000 ft regime in a covering position, looking for an option to enter into the fight.'

The engagement quickly turned into a single-circle fight, where both aircraft attempted to out-turn each other in what looked like a constant spiral, but 'Rico' held the advantage because he had managed to get behind the bandit's '3-9 line' [the imaginary line that stretches from the left wing to the right wing] in the first couple of turns.

'He recognised that I was there, and I think that he may have even visually seen "Mole" up there. The fight now turned into a left-hand descending spiral, with me having an energy advantage that I converted into a WEZ (close to within firing parameters). I spent time inside his turning circle with a high heading-crossing angle, then I flushed to the outside of his turning circle, before regaining energy, aligning circles and coming back inside his circle, looking to use an AIM-9 against him. As I cut back inside for the shot, there was an opportunity for "Mole" to come in and take a shot too, but I opted to call him off and continue my pursuit. We were now below 1000 ft.

'He tried to fly a split-s manoeuvre in what looked to me like a "cobra" [a high angle-of-attack pitch-up or pitch-down]. I came out of the fight and dipped my wings to pick up the Tally-Ho [visual contact], at which point he impacted the ground. He hit the desert floor and then tumbled with all the momentum he had for what seemed like several miles. Meanwhile, "Mole" and I were getting the "hell out of Dodge". "Mole" called, "Snap south. I'm tactical right side", and I looked left and there he was, directing our separation.'

Upon their return from their successful 19 January engagement with the IrAF, the 58th TFS's 'Citgo' flight was repeatedly locked up by Saudi F-15s flying goalkeeper CAP as they headed for Tabuk. Genuinely concerned that fratricide may occur if nothing was done about the situation, Rodriguez called AWACS and told them that if he or his flight was locked up one more time he would engage the Saudi Eagles himself! (*Ian Black via Author*)

Short of fuel, and calling for a tanker to come north, the pair retreated under the cover of 'Citgo 13' and '14' (Capt Mike 'Fish' Fisher and Capt Pat 'Pat-O' Moylan), who had raced north from the HVA CAP track to provide support.

'Citgo's' return home was disrupted by Saudi F-15 'Goalie' CAPs trying to run intercepts on them, and by a very close call with low fuel.

Rodriguez was content in the knowledge that not only had he just flown the only real turning fight of the entire war, but that he'd foiled the IrAF's best attempts to down a Coalition fighter at the same time. He believes that the MiGs originated from a covert highway airstrip known as F1, which served as an alert strip out in the desert.

On the northern front, two IrAF Mirage F 1EQs fell victim to two young Bitburg pilots on the third day of the war during the Incirlik composite wing's first daylight mission of the conflict. *Desert Storm* kills 11 and 12 were claimed by Capt David 'Spyro' Prather (in F-15C 79-0069) and Lt David Sveden (in F-15C 79-0021) during a sweep of Kirkuk airfield, north of Baghdad. Two F-15 four-ships – call-signs 'Rambo' and 'Conan' – were tasked with escorting 16 F-16s on an attack against Kirkuk's military airfield complex. Additionally, a third Incirlik F-15 four-ship ('Lobo') would provide HVA CAP.

'Rambo' flight was led by Capt Steve 'Gunga' Dingy, a recent FWS graduate who had chosen this call-sign over the ATO-generated 'JJ' 'handle' because it was one of those used by the Weapons School back home. His wingman was Capt Larry 'Von' Ludwig and his Nos 3 and 4 were Prather and Sveden. 'Conan' and 'Rambo' flew a wall formation two minutes ahead of the F-16s, and they were joined by a small contingent of F-4Gs for SAM suppression. This sortie was the first daylight mission not to be cancelled by poor weather in the north.

David Sveden recalled:

'We were about 20 miles ahead of the strikers, headed south, in the high 20s [thousand feet] and at 0.9 Mach, covering about nine miles per minute. We were in a wall formation, with a two-mile spacing between each jet, and a five-mile separation between us and "Conan", who was to our east. "Rambo" was on the west side and I was on the far west of the formation, with No 3 to my east, then Nos 1 and 2.'

With the formation set, the wall of Eagles pushed towards the target area at 1243 hrs precisely. The push point was some 50 miles north of the Turkey/Iraq border, and the F-15s did not initially detect enemy fighter activity on their radars as they swept south. Even so, AWACS was constantly broadcasting the movements of two bandits flying a CAP 15 miles northeast of Qarrayah West military airfield, south of Mosul and west of Kirkuk. Sveden continues:

'Our plan was to fly southeast to Kirkuk, and the only deviation to our flight path was going to be to avoid known SAM sites. Our job was complicated by the fact that we were flying past three active Iraqi airfields which were supposed to have been hit by now, but were actually untouched because weather had cancelled the missions tasked to take them out. So, we were concerned that we might be trapping MiGs in our "six" as we headed south. We started to see the bandits AWACS had been calling on radar, then we lost them as they turned away from us. They gradually drifted further and further right on our scopes because of our flight geometry, and at 40 miles "Gunga" decided to turn our four-ship towards them and honour the threat.

'We made a drastic right turn to the southwest, which placed me ahead of Nos 1 and 2 and inline with No 3.'

Having observed the lack of a threat over Kirkuk, Dingy instructed 'Conan' to continue southeast, while 'Rambo' prosecuted the bandits.

'Now we had made the turn, I was on the north side of the formation on a 250-degree heading. The bandits were going the same way as we were, but as they turned back towards us, I started to see a blob on the screen, rather than two individual breakouts. I took a lock because I'd been tasked to EID any guys who we may have to shoot. Our ROE said that the lack of an IFF "squawk" and an AWACS "bandit" confirmation was enough to allow us to shoot BVR. Because AWACS has been calling them bandits all along, and I was interrogating their IFF without response, I was fairly confident that we were going to be able to shoot.'

As he processed his EID at 22 miles' separation, Sveden reminded Lead that the plan had been to jettison external tanks when they closed to within 25 miles of any bandits. He then punched off his own tanks.

'Everyone blew their tanks – we had no centreline tanks that day – and shortly afterwards, Nos 1 and 3 started to get a breakout on the two bandits. In my view, No 3 then demonstrated the best comm and execution of any of the F-15 kills – as cool as you could possibly be, he called, "'Rambo 3' has a side-side breakout on the nose for 20". No 1 came back and said, "'Rambo 1', same". Then No 3 responded, "'Rambo 3', sorted side at 7000", followed by, "'Rambo 1', same, 9000". So they had individual bandits, and they know their altitudes. I'm was there (north) thinking that I had the same guy as No 1 because my bandit had the same altitude.

When IrAF fighters attempted to escape to Iran en masse in late January 1991, the 525th TFS became directly involved in the air war from its base in Incirlik. (*USAF*)

'I was actually cross-locked, taking the southern guy instead of the northern guy, but because No 1 was behind and four miles south of me, and the bandit was heading straight at me, I was in the best position to take the shot. We got to 15 miles and I wondered why we were not shooting at them. "Gunga" queried the AWACS controller, "Understand bandit?!", but I must have heard AWACS say "bandit" about four times by now! Well, these guys ('Rambo' flight) were much more experienced in working with AWACS than I, and knew that AWACS would call everyone "bandit" in exercises like *Red Flag*. They wanted to hear AWACS say it one more time to be sure.'

As the bandits closed to within 15 miles, with their noses pointed straight at him, Sveden became increasingly concerned. He watched his RWR for indications of a spike, but nothing happened. Nothing, that is, until the gap closed to 12 miles:

'The tone startled me. I was looking inside the cockpit at the RWR, trying to interpret what I was seeing, but I was thinking that this whole thing was stupid – I had this guy locked, he was not "squawking", AWACS had called him a bandit and I knew that he was a bandit. So I shot him. I hit the pickle button and shot the first missile of my life (Sveden had only 180 hours in the jet at this time). The AIM-7 came off and I saw it fly out. I then visually checked to the south to see that No 3 had an AIM-7 in the air too. I could now see my bandit, so I was concentrating on keeping a tally-ho on him.

'My guy manoeuvred to the north, almost to a beam aspect, but "Spyro's" guy stayed head-on. My guy may have been following GCI directions, and as I bored in on him, I was fully expecting to have to fire again – he looked just like an F-16 pilot doing a radar missile defence. At about four miles the bandit pitched back into me, but that was far too early, as I had room to shoot my second AIM-7.

'About three seconds after I fired the second weapon, the first missile got there. There was a flash in the TD box and the missile detonated close enough to take his tail off. His jet started cart-wheeling end-over-end and breaking apart. Then my second missile guided into the fireball. Simultaneously, "Spyro's" missiles impacted his bandit.

'I still didn't know what type of aircraft I'd shot down, and as we continued to head towards Qarrayah West, I started to prepare to blow through past the airfield, working our short-range radar game plan and going to Auto Guns to acquire any pop-up contacts.

'Unbeknownst to me at the time though, No 1 had dropped 8000 lbs of gas with his two wing tanks because they had not fed, so he was looking at 6600 lbs of gas on his fuel gauge – well below what he wanted to see. He called a turn to the north to get out of Iraq. As I rolled wings level, I looked over my left wing and saw a Mirage missing a tail pointed straight at

Back home at Incirlik and ready to celebrate following their 19 January Mirage F 1EQ kills, 'Rambo' flight pose for the camera. These 525th TFS pilots are, from left to right, David Sveden, David Prather, Larry Ludwig and Steve Dingy. (*David Sveden via Author*)

the ground. That was the first time I knew what I'd shot down.'

Reforming with the rest of the formation, Sveden was initially confused when he saw that Prather was missing three AIM-7s. It later became apparent that Prather's first AIM-7 had 'gone stupid', flying off to the right, so he had followed up with two more in rapid succession at eight and seven miles.

Whilst researching this kill, the author has learned that US Intelligence was monitoring the F 1EQ intra-flight communication frequency. The Mirages were operating as call-sign 'Lion' flight, with the lead jet being flown by a major and a junior lieutenant flying the second F 1. The two argued amongst themselves as to whether or not to engage the F-15s, whom they knew were bearing down on them. The reluctant major, to the north (left side) of the formation, wanted to run from the fight, and it was he who died first when Prather's second AIM-7 impacted his aircraft.

The bolder lieutenant observed his leader's destruction and called to GCI, '"Lion 1" is no more'. Moments later the tail of his own Mirage was severed by Sveden's first AIM-7. The Mirages had been flying a line abreast split of two to three miles up until the lieutenant's missile defence to the north. Neither pilot attempted ejection.

David Sveden is seen in the cockpit of F-15C 79-0069 in mid-1992. His flightmate David Prather claimed his Mirage F 1EQ kill in this jet on 19 January 1991. The 525th TFS was inactivated on 1 April 1992 and its pilots and aircraft were transferred to the wing's 22nd TFS, hence the 'Stinger' patch on Sveden's helmet visor cover.
(*David Sveden via Author*)

MiG-23 KILLS

26 January saw Capt Rhory 'Hoser' Draeger (in F-15C 85-0108) and his wingmen, Capt Tony 'Kimo' Schiavi (in F-15C 85-0104) and Capt Cesar 'Rico' Rodriguez (in F-15C 85-0114) each down a MiG-23 'Flogger'. They were Draeger's and Rodriguez's second kills, and came when four 'Floggers' attempted to relocate to Baghdad, and the sanctuary of its 'Super MEZ'. Schiavi recalled:

'For this particular day we changed our original paired four-ship of Draeger as No 1, me as No 2, Chuck Magill as No 3 and Mark Arriola as No 4, to Rhory Draeger and me, Cesar Rodriguez at No 3 and Bruce 'Roto' Till at No 4. We were assigned a HVA protection mission north of the border in the western sector between Baghdad and the H2/H3 airfield complex.'

The weather was good on the 26th, with only a few layers of mid-level cloud and a low-level overcast. The four jets took off following afternoon launch, and received fuel from a tanker south of the border, Schiavi recalled:

'The first part of the mission was uneventful and quiet. It was mentally challenging from the start, however, because our mission required us to know where all the friendly aircraft were. Prior to taking off, we had spent hours learning and studying the ATO, and that in turn allowed us to position ourselves in support of other flights once we got out there.'

As 'Citgo' flight cycled to and from the tanker in pairs, there were overlaps – short periods of time when the whole four-ship was on the CAP station simultaneously, before two jets had to leave for the tanker.

'It was just as "Rico" and "Roto" left to get more gas that AWACS called to say that it had MiGs airborne from H2/H3 in western Iraq, headed for Baghdad (Rodriguez recalled that the AWACS was initially unsure if the target was a single MiG, or a car travelling at high speed). At the time we were headed south, and "Hoser" decided that we needed to get our four-ship back together again before we went north after these guys.

'The geometry was such that the MiGs were some 80 miles in front of us by the time we achieved this, but "Hoser", being the talented and smart guy that he was, asks AWACS if we could follow them anyway. These guys were headed towards the "Super MEZ", which was not a place you wanted to go flying through, but there was plenty of time before we got to that point, and we didn't know that these guys would not turn back south at some stage. "Hoser" was one of those guys who always thought ahead – "How could this thing turn out differently?" – whereas the traditional view would have been, "Hey, we're in an 80-mile tail chase with these guys. Why are we even wasting the gas?".'

As Draeger's flight approached the SAM rings outside Baghdad, AWACS called to say that it had another flight of four MiGs taking off right behind the first group.

'That put us in a geometry situation, because we had four MiGs in front of us at about 70 miles and another four at out left "seven o'clock" – we could have quickly found ourselves sandwiched between the two. "Hoser" reacted immediately, ordering a delayed four-ship 90-degree left turn to almost exactly 270 degrees, placing the new MiG-23 contacts right on our nose.'

The F-15s bore down on the 'Floggers' in a wall formation, with Schiavi furthest north in No 2 position and Draeger at No 1 to his left. Rodriguez was No 3 to Draeger's left and Till No 4, farthest south.

Aware that the IrAF had lost the will to fight, and would turn tail as soon as a RWR indication showed they were being engaged, Draeger had briefed that he wanted to stay in 'raw' radar search mode (RWS) so that the gap could be closed until the MiGs could not escape.

'We do not want to get into any turning merges with anyone if we did not have to, so we get our MiG-23 EID and AWACS clearances out of the way well before we could shoot. The MiGs were at 500 ft, and we were flying a cut-off intercept on them. At about 40 miles, AWACS told us that one of the MiGs has returned home, so we now had a radar picture of a three-aircraft "Vic" – one guy out front and the other two guys flying behind and either side of him.'

On Alert at Tabuk during *Desert Storm*, Bruce Till, Tony Schiavi and the doughty Rhory Draeger pose for the camera. When providing the author with a copy of this photograph, Schiavi commented, 'Notice "Hoser's" ever present golf club in the corner and our nice "blackout curtains". Who said pilots can't improvise!' (*Tony Schiavi via Author*)

Rodriguez added that RC-135 *Rivet Joint* also confirmed the EID on the MiG-23s. Draeger ordered a jettison of wing tanks to allow superior manoeuvrability and greater speed with which to increase their WEZ.

'We were doing about Mach 1.2, coming downhill at the MiGs, and we didn't think that we would be able to see them because there was a bit of an undercast below us', Schiavi recalled. Rodriguez added:

'The first issue was, "were we going to be able to see these guys visually through that undercast?" At about 25 miles, there was this "sucker hole" that we could see through, so we all converged within a mile of each other to try and squeeze through it – we scared ourselves doing that. At 18,000 ft, the sucker hole started to expand and we now had room to manoeuvre.'

Schiavi continued:

'"Hoser" then called a targeting plan – he was going to take the pointy end of the "Vic", targeting me on the northern trailer and "Rico" and "Roto" on the other trailer to the south. We were fortunate that over the desert environment we were not getting too much ground clutter, and we could break the MiGs out on radar with ease.'

Next, Draeger ordered Nos 3 and 4 to execute a check turn to create separation following the formation's unintentional compression as they penetrated the weather. Wary that the AIM-7 liked to pull lead on its target, and that the check turn placed his second element slightly behind him, he also had the presence of mind to warn Till to be careful not to fire his AIM-7s at a time when they might fly towards and into him. 'No 4, don't shoot through me', Draeger transmitted.

Schiavi recalled:

'Up until now, things had been very calm – you would have almost thought that we were flying a training mission over the Gulf of Mexico from our home base in Florida. "Hoser" shot an AIM-7 first (at 11 miles), but his missile had a motor no-fire. He shot again, and the Sparrow headed towards the lead "Flogger". By now we were calling, "Tally-Ho", on the MiGs, and we saw "Hoser's" missile hit the back end of the aeroplane. There was only a small explosion and a dust cloud, but "Hoser" called, "Splash 1 from 1". When he saw the "Flogger" fly through the explosion, he selected an AIM-9 and set off after him.'

Trailing smoke, the MiG-23 turned north.

'Just as "Hoser" was about to fire an AIM-9 at his "Flogger", it began to fall apart. Its engine caught fire and eventually its fuel cells exploded, leaving another charred streak on the desert floor.

'Listening to the cockpit audio tape, you could tell that the adrenaline was now pumping, because as soon as aeroplanes started blowing up, everyone's voice went up about six octaves!

'I fired about seven or eight seconds after "Hoser", and I used two missiles because I was coming in at an angle, and my target was low. I also wanted to be sure that the MiG died. We came down very fast through some clouds and moist air, so we were trailing condensation and wing-tip streamers – the MiG pilots saw this and began a hard right-hand turn into us. At that instant my first missile hit the front of the second MiG and it basically vapourised. My second missile went right through the fireball.'

Tony Schiavi and his crew chief stand in front of F-15C 85-0104 (the jet in which the former scored his 'Flogger' kill on 26 January 1991) just 24 hours before returning to the USA following the completion of *Desert Storm*.
(*Tony Schiavi via Author*)

Rodriguez and Till had simultaneously engaged the final MiG. The latter pilot shot first, but his first AIM-7 hung, the second missile experienced a motor no-fire and his third impacted only seconds after Rodriguez's AIM-7 hit the target. Rodriguez recounted:

'I fired two AIM-7s which both proceed inbound towards their targets. My weapon hit at the same time as "Kimo's" missile hit his target. "Boom!" The MiGs were about 400 ft above the ground and the fireball charred the desert floor (three to four miles south of Draeger's MiG wreckage).'

The charred streaks and scattered remains from the trailing 'Floggers' 'straddled' the main highway from H3 to Baghdad, serving as testimony to the Eagle's complete dominance for weeks to come.

Schiavi concluded:

'We came off north, away from the fireballs, because we just wanted to get the hell out of there as fast as we could. We turned south and punched off our remaining fuel tanks, but we were critically low on fuel. The tanker, God bless him, came north across the border to meet us, allowing us to get back home to Tabuk, rather than having to divert to another airfield. We went with "Roto" to an unused area near the base and he jettisoned his hung AIM-7, then we flew victory rolls over the base and came in for a full-stop landing with all the maintenance guys on the base there to meet us.'

The ability to get to the tanker so quickly is in no small part down to the fact that as 'Citgo' executed the intercept, Draeger and Rodriguez had told AWACS they would soon be short of fuel.

Sadly, in 1995, Maj Rhory 'Hoser' Draeger was killed in a car accident. Many have paid homage to him, and Tony Schiavi's tribute echoes the sentiment of them all:

'He was a pilot, warrior, officer and great man from whom you could learn *so* much. He always had supreme SA – no matter how hectic things were. I am just thankful that I had the opportunity to fly with him, and I credit a lot of the skills that I have developed over the years to him. He was hard, too. I flew with him a lot before the war, and I remember coming back from one particular *Desert Shield* mission, when we'd dropped down low to practice SAM and AAA

Tony Schiavi's F-15C 85-0104 is seen on the wing not long after its return to Eglin AFB. Delivered to the USAF on 24 October 1986, this aircraft served with the 33rd TFW until passed on to the 3rd Wing's 19th FS in July 1998. The jet still remains operational with the unit at Elmendorf AFB, Alaska, today. (*Ted Carlson*)

'Rockin' the Camel'. Double MiG killer Jay Denney (left) of the 53rd TFS teams up with an unsuspecting Camel and fellow Eagle pilot Jethro Miller to form an impromptu rock band at 'PSAB'. This photo was taken by Bob Hehemann, who went on to score no less than three kills. (*Jay Denney via Author*)

Minus his guitar and camel, Jay Denney (top right in baseball cap) enjoys some downtime at 'PSAB' with other Bitburg pilots. (*Jay Denney via Author*)

evasion, and I was having one of those days when my formation flying was not on. He was getting pretty upset with me to the point that he radioed, "Two, if you don't stay in position I'm sending you home"! That was how he was, and although I was mad at him for talking to me like that, I knew that he was trying to make me better.

'You strive for perfection every time you fly, but with "Hoser" I just tried that much harder.'

BITBURG KILLS

On 27 January, the 53rd TFS's Capts Jay Denney (in F-15C 84-0025) and Ben 'Coma' Powell (in F-15C 84-0027) conducted what was arguably the most successful single engagement of the war, resulting in the destruction of four IrAF fighters. The mission was also noteworthy because it demonstrated that the Iraqis still possessed some form of coherent IADS ten days into the war. The Eagle pilots also got closer to Baghdad itself than any previous F-15C crews. Denney recalled:

'Our four-ship showed up at our CAP station south of the border, and we checked in with "Bulldog" (AWACS), who immediately tasked us to "Charlotte" CAP, 75 miles southwest of Baghdad. Once there, an hour or so passed before we got a "snap" to a pair of bogeys southeast of Baghdad. "Coma" and I pressed towards them, past Al Amara, where there were SA-3s, and ending up in a 40-mile tail chase against an adversary who was clearly "husbanding" (pulling back to Baghdad) and did not want to fight.

'With fuel becoming more of a consideration, we pulled back to 30 miles southeast of Al Amara to watch them for 15 minutes, before Nos 3 and 4 replaced us and we went to get gas. By the time it was there turn to get gas, another "snap" had come in – "Bullseye 130 for 80", which was east of Nasiriyah and north of Basra. The bogeys were headed northwest, so we made a hard right turn and pressed. Everyone else on frequency started looking for them too. I called the contact to "Bulldog", and as he handed them off to us, the AUX frequency was full with all of the other F-15s calling up to say, "good luck"!'

Believing that they were dealing with a simple element of two Iraqi fighters, Denney refined his interception:

'They were down at about 5000 ft, headed northwest at 350 knots calibrated. We were east-bound, trying to cut them off. When we got inside 20 miles, they turned out to be northeast bound, heading for the Iranian border, so we stayed up at 30,000 ft at Mach 1.1 in full AB, trying to get the closure (before they crossed the border). As they turned northeast, I told "Coma" to "Break lock and don't spike them", because I didn't want to give them notice that we were chasing them down.

'We had got to within 15 miles when they made a turn back towards Baghdad, giving us a geometry cut-off. The first contact to turn was the western one, and the eastern one trailed in a four-mile echelon formation to the northwest. I was to the east and my wingman was to the west, and we ramped down on these guys with about 300 knots overtake. As we continued to close, we went through our ID matrix. AWACS called, "Bandit, Bandit, cleared to fire", and we were now just trying to get into weapons parameters.'

Descending to 3000 ft, both F-15 pilots spied their targets' shadows.

'I was a little bit out in front of my wingman, so I took the first AIM-7 shot at about six miles. I got a good fly-out and lock, the missile going right to him, but I didn't actually see it fuse. The best guess we have is that it did not fuse in time and the warhead exploded into the sand below him. If it did fuse, the warhead damage was not enough to stop him flying. "Coma" employed an AIM-7 at his target, and at this point in time we *still* thought that we had just two single contacts. I watched his missile fly out at the same time as my MiG started a gentle left turn at about 2G. As he did so, I selected an AIM-9 and shot within two miles – it hit him directly, and the explosion looked like a Molotov cocktail because he was low, the desert was flat and he was full of jet fuel.'

Denney was down to 3000 ft when Powell's AIM-7 also missed.

'He immediately called "Tally Two". He was well above me on my left at about 12,000 ft, and had a better view than I. I too looked over to the left and saw his group – I spotted one MiG, and as I kept scanning from left-to-right I saw another on my right. I called, "Confirmed, Tally Two. I'm engaging north".'

Unaware that there had been more than two MiGs from the start, Denney was actually talking at crossed purposes with Powell. Powell's 'Tally Two' call came because he had visually discerned that his single target was actually a MiG-23 and Mirage F 1EQ in fingertip (extremely close) formation. The call prompted Denney, however, to re-scan his own horizon, allowing him to pick up the wingman to the MiG-23 that he had just shot down himself.

F-15C 84-0027 was used by 53rd TFS pilot Capt Ben Powell to claim a MiG-23 and a Mirage F 1EQ destroyed on 27 January 1991. Initially delivered new to the 33rd TFW's 58th TFS on 1 June 1986, this aircraft served with the 36th TFW from December 1988 until September 1998, when it moved with the 53rd FS to 52nd FW control. The fighter was transferred from Spangdahlem, in Germany, to the 493rd FS/48th FW at RAF Lakenheath in October 2001, where it remains today. (*Author / FJPhotography.com*)

'Powell rolled upside down, shot a second Sparrow and killed one of them. I was now about 3000 ft to the east of this, and as the first one blew up, I saw the seat come out, the 'chute open and the pilot fall straight into the fireball on the ground after just one swing. Almost immediately the third MiG blew up and fell apart. I was now looking at the fourth guy to the northeast, who had entered a left turn. I ordered Powell, who was still off to my left, to come right as I descended to 300 ft, with the MiG at just 50 ft. I couldn't get a radar lock, so I uncaged my AIM-9. As I went to fire he reversed, leaving me with a simple, "dead-six" AIM-9 shot right in the behind. The missile came off and hit him. leaving me just a half-mile behind the explosion that followed.

'We were now about 40 miles outside of Baghdad, and we could see some of the city buildings from where we were. We were starting to approach "SAMPAC-2" (part of the "Super MEZ"), but we had not experienced any SAM indications up till then. However, when the second the fourth MiG blew up everything came online, and our RWR recorded a frenzy of activity – they had been holding off so that they did not shoot their own guys down. We were in their WEZ, so we did a hard right to the south, stayed low, punched off our wing tanks and got the hell out of there. We eventually got fuel from a tanker which had come 75 miles north of the border to meet us. We got gas and continued to CAP for a few hours more.'

SOESTERBERG KILL

The Soesterberg F-15 unit claimed its first kill on 28 January, when Capt Donald S Watrous (in 22nd TFS jet F-15C 79-0022), flying on the wing of Capt Gary 'Baghwan' Bauman (Bauman was not the squadron's weapons officer, as is widely reported), downed a MiG-23 during a barrier CAP patrol over eastern Iraq.

These BARCAP missions were intended to cut off IrAF access to the safety of Iran. Iraqi pilots had, by this stage, lost the determination to fight, and were being driven by self-preservation. In the engagement that followed, Watrous and Bauman experienced the fog of war, and were unfortunate enough to have almost nothing go right.

Watrous' two-ship was in the process of relieving another F-15 CAP when two MiG-23s made a run for the border. The timing of the dash was probably set to coincide with the F-15s' handover so as to create maximum confusion.

The pilots observed the two contacts in RWS and assumed that they were a south-bound two-ship in an azimuth spread. In fact they were actually a lead-trail two-ship with a 90-degree aspect, heading east to Iran. This assumption probably stemmed from peacetime training, when adversary fighters often used an azimuth spread, but it could have quickly been resolved had one of the two F-15 pilots quickly locked up the contacts and sampled the additional data generated by STT. This would have told them that the fighters were headed east, and would have allowed them to make a left turn to cut them off. However, instead of pulling lead to gain closure, the Eagle pilots continued pointing at the MiGs, and ended up in a dreaded tail-chase scenario.

Sniper scopes were fitted to many F-15Cs during *Desert Storm* to allow early identification of aircraft that were still beyond the visual acuity of the human eyeball. This particular example is seen bolted onto the cockpit coaming of a 1st TFW jet at Dhahran. (*Ian Black via Author*)

Donald Watrous' MiG-29-killing mount F-15C 79-0022 now serves with the Oregon Air National Guard (ANG). Transferred to the 22nd TFS/36th TFW in August 1993, this aircraft was passed on to the 1st FS/325th FTW in January 1994. Five years later, in March 1999, the fighter joined the ANG's Oregon-based 114th FS. It recently returned to frontline use with the 325th FTW at Tyndall AFB, in Florida. (*Gary Klett via Author*)

Watrous engaged his afterburner and was soon travelling as fast as his fully-loaded Eagle would go, but he was still unable to close the gap. He finally decided to get rid of his external tanks, jettisoning them at 630 knots. Unfortunately, a small warning in the F-15 flight manual prohibited the simultaneous jettison of wing stores above 600 knots, and it quickly became apparent why. Both tanks dropped down into the slip stream and immediately came back up against the bottom of each wing. One punctured the bottom of one wing and the other ripped the outer three feet off the wingtip! Watrous had no idea this had happened – he simply knew that his clean F-15C was now gaining on the trailing MiG-23.

Col(Ret) Doug 'Disco' Dildy, who later flew with Bauman, and was told the story of the engagement by him, recalled that simultaneously, 'Baghwan was actually chasing a "Fishbed" which was running down winding valleys at extremely low altitude. The two IrAF aircraft had split up and were dashing individually for the sanctuary of Iran. However, he got a VID from more than a couple of miles out on a very small target manoeuvring frenetically down the winding gorges. His radar eventually transferred to the ground before he was in range for a shot and he lost the lock, the visual and the opportunity for his own kill'.

Once in range to shoot the 'Flogger', Watrous suffered no fewer three AIM-7 motor no-fires, and inexperience got the better of him – because he had never fired a missile before, he was unaware that each round had failed to light and guide. He therefore waited for the countdown in the HUD to reach zero before firing his second, third and fourth missiles, allowing the 'Flogger' to get closer and close to Iran. His fourth Sparrow finally lit, guided and killed the running MiG, and there is speculation that the wreckage may have actually fallen in Iran.

Well below Bingo fuel, Watrous headed back to the tanker, where the boomer noticed the major damage to the jet. Watrous landed successfully back at Incirlik, but it was the last time that F-15C 79-0022 flew in the war!

On 29 January, Capt David Rose (in F-15C 85-0102), attached to the 59th TFS from the 60th TFS 'Crows', scored kill number 21 when he participated in an OCA sortie. His MiG-23 kill probably came from his second AIM-7 shot, as the first missile reportedly experienced fusing problems.

Following three days of inactivity for the F-15Cs, 2 February saw the 36th TFW's Capt Greg Masters (in 79-0064) score the only Il-76 kill of the war. He provided the author with the following diary entry, written on the evening of his kill. He was flying as lead in a four-ship

OCA sweep that included Capts Rich Fullerton, H M Hepperlin and Mike Rockel:

'Well, I think I shot down one of my beloved enemies today. I was air-to-air mission commander, and had eight F-15s and four F-16s at my disposal to protect a large F-16 strike force attacking an airfield south of Kirkuk, as well as other high-value airborne assets north of the border. We also had to cut off aircraft attempting to escape into Iran.

'My four-ship was flying BARCAP east of Kirkuk and west of the Iranian border, prior to the strike package pushing across the Turkey/Iraq border, when my No 4 got a radar contact at 4000 ft. We chased him down as he headed west toward Kirkuk. His route was obscured by cloud, and he had remained below our radar coverage up until the point when we detected him. We were five miles behind him, and closing fast, by the time I ascertained that he was not a friendly and shot my first AIM-7 Sparrow. I jettisoned my external wing tanks and prepared to follow up with a second shot, but the first missile guided perfectly. Because he was below a cloud deck, we didn't see the explosion, and the kill is not (yet) confirmed. However, my No 4's radar and mine both went "mem" (lost the target) when the missile timed out, and after we turned around and came back, we couldn't find him, so we are fairly sure we got him.

'Efforts are being made to confirm the kill. I am mission commander again for a similar flight tomorrow.'

No fewer than four IrAF jets we claimed by the 53rd TFS on 6 February, when Capt Thomas 'Vegas' Dietz (in F-15C 79-0078) and Lt Robert 'Gigs' Hehemann (in F-15C 84-0019) got in amongst formations of Su-25s and MiG-21s. Like Tollini and Pitts, Draeger and Schiavi, and Williams and Graeter, Dietz and Hehemann were part of a paired four-ship which had flown together extensively in the months leading up to the war.

By early February, the omnipresent F-15 force was no longer tied to particular packages, but allowed to roam within sets of coordinates to allow optimum flexibility. Indeed, in the week prior to their quadruple kills on 6 February, Dietz and Hehemann had engaged two MiG-25 'Foxbats' *directly* over the heart of Baghdad.

On the 6th, the 53rd TFS was tasked with providing Eagles to execute 24-hour roving patrols of four F-15 four-ships which encircled

Two 32nd FS F-15Cs perform a flyby at Soesterberg in the early summer of 1990. The aircraft in the background (79-0032) was one of 24 F-15Cs hastily supplied to the RSAF in September 1990 as part of the *Desert Shield* build up. F-15C 81-0046 deployed with the 32nd TFS to *Desert Storm*, and remained with the unit until transferred to the 95th FS/325th FTW in August 1992. It still serves with the training unit today. (*Bob Archer*)

Baghdad and cut off the IrAF's escape routes to the north and the east. Dietz and Hehemann were on one of these missions that day, the former recalling:

'We were on our CAP station to the east, right on the edge of the Iranian border, when AWACS told us that it had Iraqi aircraft north of Baghdad, approaching at low altitude, east-south-east. We oriented ourselves in that direction and picked them up on our radar, beginning an intercept to see if we can get them before they reach the

border. "Gigs" – who has only 100 hours in the aeroplane, and was a very young, but very talented, guy – and I were Nos 3 and 4 on "Cindy" CAP, while our squadron commander, Randy "Bigs" Biggum, and Lynn "Boo Boo" Broome were at the tanker getting gas.'

As the F-15 pilots committed against the contacts (two MiG-21s and two Su-25s), AWACS attempted to attain a positive identification, freeing the Eagles up to inspect the local airspace with greater scrutiny.

'We sanitised the airspace around the contacts and then, in accordance with our training, melded our radars so that we were looking at the same radar picture. "Gigs" then took one group (northern) and I took the other (southern). We started at 33,000 ft and descended from 50 miles away, getting clearance to fire before we got to visual range, and having punched through a cloud deck. We locked them up and took our first shots with plenty of closure on them. Following our missiles, I got a tally on two guys at low altitude and in close formation – maybe 100 ft apart. To this day I have no idea what happened to my AIM-7, so I rolled in behind them somewhere inside of two miles and I shot an (uncaged) AIM-9 at each bandit – as the AIM-9s streaked away about two seconds apart, it looked like they were almost flying formation on each other.

'It was easy in this environment to get temporal distortion, and everything seemed to slow down – the missiles guided as advertised, flying straight to the aircraft. I saw the warheads detonate, but then nothing. It looked like they had had no effect on these guys. The next thing that I noticed was a trickle of flame emanating from the aircraft on the left, followed by a second trickle of flame from the jet on the right. A few seconds later both aircraft impacted the desert floor, resulting in fireballs erupting across the desert like napalm. There were no parachutes that I could see.

'It then occurred to me that this had been too easy, and that I needed to find my wingman, and any other aircraft out there. I looked to the left and spotted a jet very close to me, with its nose pointed out in front of me, in the same plane of motion as me, and in a set-up where he could conceivably shoot his gun at me. As my brain processed this, it became clear to me that this aeroplane was on fire, its canopy was gone – the guy had ejected – and that "Gigs" had shot

Photographed at Robins AFB, Georgia, in 2003, F-15C 79-0078 has been incorrectly credited with the destruction of two 'MiG-22' aircraft! This machine was actually used by the 53rd TFS's Thomas Dietz to down two MiG-21s on 6 February 1991. Following 13 years of service with the 36th TFW, 79-0078 transferred to the 3rd Wing's 54th FS in August 1994. It remained in Alaska until passed on to the 58th FS/33rd FW at Eglin in October 1998, and the fighter is still in service with the unit today. (*Randall Haskin via Author*)

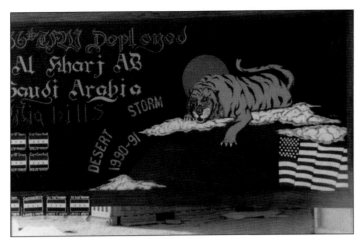

Believed to have been painted by Capt John Doneski, the 53rd TFS's kill board is seen prior to 20 March 1991, showing the eight kills scored up to that point in the conflict by Hehemann, Dietz, Powell and Denney. On 20 March Doneski claimed a kill himself, and two days later Dietz and Hehemann added two more to the unit tally. (*Bob Hehemann via Author*)

him. Even further to the left, I saw the wreckage of another guy he'd shot soon after the jet had hit the ground.'

'Gigs' Hehemann narrated the events as seen from his cockpit:

'The Iraqis were in a lead-trail formation from our perspective, but they were actually in echelon. I took the northern group and

locked the northernmost guy at the north side of the formation. "Vegas" cut underneath me to get to the northern group, and at that point I decided that I didn't need my radar. I could see one guy, so I thumbed back to AIM-9 and let the first missile rip at him. As the missile was in the air I picked up another guy to the right, so I pointed my nose at him, and with about 490 knots on the airspeed, inside of a mile, shot a second missile. I then picked up a third guy – just as I was about to "pickle" (a third AIM-9), he turned into a fireball – he turned out to be the second guy that "Vegas" had targeted.

'I looked back at the first guy that I had shot at, and it reminded me of someone taking a lit cigarette and scraping it along concrete – a trail of burning embers on the ground. The second guy was still flying, but right then the AIM-9 impacted the engine and the explosion cut the aeroplane in half. That big, straight "Frogfoot" wing just flat-planed in the wind, the tail came off and the aeroplane immediately slowed. It then started to yaw, and ended up with its nose pointed at me, looking like it could threaten me. I sharpened my right turn and picked "Vegas" up at my right "three o'clock".'

From the first AIM-9 fired to the last Iraqi jet exploding took no more than 15 seconds.

The following day, the 58th TFS's Capt Anthony R 'ET' Murphy (in F-15C 85-0102) and Col Rick Parsons (in F-15C

RAF Lakenheath's 493rd FS now operates the airframe that Greg Hehemann used to claim his 6 February 1991 Su-25 kills. 84-0019 wears its kill markings with pride. (*Author/FJPhotography.com*)

An IrAF Su-25K is seen on display during the Defence Exhibition in Baghdad in 1989. By 1991, some 40 survivors of the 80 examples reportedly delivered in 1986–88 were operated by Nos 114 and 118 Sqns. A considerable number of these were located at Tallil AB, in southern Iraq. Two were shot down by USAF F-15Cs and seven flown out to Iran. (*US DoD via Tom Cooper*)

84-0124) claimed three more kills for the Eagle force. A section of two F-15Cs were flying BARCAP along the Iraq/Iran border when they engaged and destroyed a gaggle of escaping Su-7/22 'Fitters' in a rear-aspect tail chase. Parsons, then 33rd TFW commander, allegedly downed the Su-7 with an AIM-9 after his wingman, Capt Murphy, destroyed the two 'Fitters' with AIM-7s. The two-ship had jettisoned their tanks and closed to within ten miles of the target group in order to bring their weapons to bear.

This engagement is somewhat enigmatic in that there are (unsubstantiated) suggestions that 'ET' scored all three kills but later 'donated' the third to Col Parsons. Indeed, the latter pilot admitted in an interview that he'd never actually witnessed his second missile (his first was beaten to its target by one of 'ET's') impact the target, but that he and Murphy later pieced together the video tape recorder system, resulting in 'the third kill being attributed to my (Parson's) missile'.

Who it was exactly that made this 'attribution' is unclear, although it is noteworthy that the original Central Command (CENTCOM) message traffic submitted immediately after the kills purportedly records Murphy as claiming three MiGs and Parsons one. It is believed that Parsons' kill was later turned down, after which Murphy 'donated' one of his three 'confirmed' kills to his boss.

Parsons returned to Eglin AFB with one kill credit painted next to his name on his jet, and the USAF Historical Research Agency's data (issued in 2001) credits him with a single Su-7 kill.

7 February also saw Bitburg pilot Maj Randy May (in F-15C 80-0003) claim a helicopter kill. He fired two AIM-7s outside of ten miles at what was claimed to be a Mi-24 'Hind' gunship. Both missiles impacted the target and fused as advertised, and May's wingman reported seeing the wreckage 'fall into a military compound'. This kill is another that is shrouded in controversy.

Several interviewees have made reference to the fact that May shot through a solid undercast, and neither he, nor his wingman, actually saw the target. There was no post-kill intelligence to correlate the destruction of the helicopter either. Long-standing rumours in the Eagle community of a car travelling down a highway

Bob Hehemann (left) and Tom Dietz congratulate each other immediately upon landing at 'PSAB', having scored two kills apiece on 6 February 1991. Note the HUD tape in Dietz's left hand and the presence of CNN and Air Force cameramen to capture the event.
(*Bob Hehemann via Author*)

With celebrations still rife, Bob Hehemann, Tom Dietz, Randy Biggum and Lynn Broome pose for a group portrait.
(*Bob Hehemann via Author*)

Sporting three victory markings and depicted some time in 1992, triple killer 85-0102 is seen participating at the large-scale *Red Flag* exercise at Nellis AFB. This aircraft has served exclusively with the 33rd FW since its delivery to the USAF in October 1986. (*Ted Carlson*)

that was killed by an AIM-7 may well stem from this event, as it was widely believed, albeit in a closely-guarded way, that May actually 'shot down' a Mercedes. This kill certainly seems to warrant some independent verification, although this is unlikely, and the truth may never be known.

On the same day, six IrAF fighters successfully made it to to Iran, but two others ran out of fuel and crashed short of the border and an additional five are reported to have crashed following attempts to land on Iranian roads and major highways.

11 February saw another helicopter fall to the F-15C when the 525th TFS's Capts Steve Dingy (in F-15C 79-0048) and Mark McKenzie (in F-15C 80-0012) downed either an Aerospatiale Puma, a Sikorsky AS-61A, or a Mi-8 'Hip' transport helicopter. Whatever its exact identify, the helicopter became the 31st USAF F-15 kill when McKenzie and Dingy engaged it with AIM-7s in a rear-aspect intercept. Positive confirmation of whose AIM-7 hit first was not possible, so CENTCOM awarded each pilot a half-kill.

POST-CEASEFIRE KILLS

The 28 February ceasefire effectively brought *Desert Storm* to an end. However, F-15 crews continued to maintain a CAP station north of Baghdad, and it was while flying such a mission on 20 March that two Eagles engaged a pair of errant Su-22s over the city of Tikrit – Saddam Hussein's home town. The 53rd TFS's Capt John Doneski (in F-15C 84-0014) intercepted the trailing jet, downing it with an AIM-9 fired from the rear hemisphere. The second Su-22 landed at Tikrit AB.

Training versions of the AIM-9 and AIM-7 await loading. The AIM-7 packed a hefty punch that shredded the aircraft against which it exploded – very often there was little left of the target, particularly if the red hot iron rods of the warhead punctured its fuel tanks. (*Author/FJPhotography.com*)

These post-war CAPs were usually quite uneventful, and the biggest enemy that threatened most F-15 pilots during this period was complacency. Drilling holes in the sky while manning CAP stations over Iraq was the most boring thing MiG killer Thomas Dietz had ever done in his life, and that meant concentration could be

Bob Hehemann's PC-9-killing F-15C 84-0015 prepares for a flight from RAF Lakenheath with the 493rd FS in 2003. It has served with the only F-15C-equipped unit in USAFE since late 1998.
(*Author/FJPhotography.com*)

84-0015 sits alongside MiG-23 and Mirage F 1EQ killer 84-0027 at Lakenheath. Airframes still serving with the USAF that have victories to their credit usually feature kill markings beneath the cockpit.
(*Author/FJPhotography.com*)

lost and mistakes made. Six weeks had passed since his double kill at the beginning of February, and Operation *Desert Storm* had now given way to Operation *Provide Comfort* – a humanitarian mission to protect and supply the impoverished Shiites and Marsh Arabs to the south and Kurds to the north.

Provide Comfort called for the Eagle pilots to enforce northern and southern no-fly zones, preventing Iraqi fixed-wing aircraft from attacking the impoverished refugees. On 22 March, Dietz was flying just such a mission in F-15C 84-0010. He recalled;

'We were just about ready to come home when we decided to investigate a few radar contacts headed west that were to the northeast of us. Normally, when we locked up a helicopter it looked like a fixed-wing target in terms of airspeed on our radar, but as the latter settled down, the airspeed indication walked its way back down to about 100 knots or so. We then knew it was a helicopter. Well, these two contacts stop at about 300 knots, so I decide that we would VID them.

'We headed northeast and then turned in behind them, sanitising the area as we went. We locked them up, and as we got into visual range, I could discern that my aircraft contact was camouflaged, had a sloped tail and a pointed nose. I thought to myself that it was definitely not a helicopter, and that it met our strict ROE.'

Dietz did well to visually identify his target aircraft (an Su-22) without a close pass, as a combination of the heavy haze that particular day and the much greener terrain in northern Iraq made visual acquisition and identification difficult. Satisfied that the ROE was met, he rolled in behind the fighter-bomber as Lt Robert Hehemann (in F-15C 84-0015) engaged his target some 1.5 miles further south.

'We had started off above them, but we were at a co-altitude of about 1000 ft when I shot the guy down with an AIM-9 at less than a mile's separation. The missile came off of the rail and flew right up the Su-22's tailpipe. It blew up just like you see in the movies, forcing me to pull out of the way to avoid this huge fireball and debris. As I rolled over to see it all, I spotted chunks of metal falling to the ground.

'Meanwhile, "Gigs" was telling me that his target was a turboprop, which we were not allowed to shoot down, but its pilot had seen my guy explode and had had enough. He ejected and came down in his parachute as "Gigs" went ripping by the Iraqi pilot at 450 knots.'

Hehemann added:

'I almost speared the guy as he ejected – he surprised the hell out of me! I checked him in his 'chute and he was alive, hanging there with his goggles on. He had punched out of a camouflaged PC-9 with rocket rails. It carried on flying perfectly straight and level, so I flew close formation with it until it started a gradual descent – it crashed one minute and fifty seconds later to be exact.'

Dietz had killed an Su-22 'Fitter' that had been bombing Kurdish civilians. The PC-9 was acting as a forward air controller, spotting targets and firing smoke markers to identify them for the 'Fitter' to then attack. These kills were the last scored against by the F-15 against the IrAF, and they were Dietz's and Hehemann's third each, making them the most successful MiG-killing duo of the war.

On 22 March 1991, the mere sight of Tom Dietz despatching a Su-22 nearby caused the pilot of a Pilatus PC-9, acting as an airborne FAC for the Sukhoi, to eject. (*Herman Potgieter*)

CONCLUSIONS

The F-15's success and, more to the point, the success of *specific* F-15 units, can be attributed to a wide range of technological, doctrinal, and local factors.

The technologies that allowed the Eagle to dominate with utter conviction are obvious – radar, on-board EID capabilities, AWACS, *Rivet Joint,* and missiles combined to reach out and subjugate the enemy with little trouble. Whilst the AIM-7M suffered a higher percentage of failures than could have been forecast, it did offer better fusing and reliability and had fewer limitations in the beam and the tail-aspect envelope than the previous AIM-7F variant of the Sparrow missile.

Combined, these capabilities and technologies permitted a tactical change in thinking in the F-15 world that stamped its mark on this conflict. That change did away with the VID mentality – where the Eagle had to turn at the merge to kill its foe – of the early 1980s, and ushered in its place a BVR mindset that promoted long-range shots that kept the Eagle away from the threatening short-range systems of the newest Russian fighters.

Although the IrAF itself was complicit in allowing the Eagle to rack up a 36:0 kill ratio – if only because it lacked the backbone to fight – there is little doubt that the outcome would not have been significantly altered had it tried a little harder.

Doctrinal influences are abundantly obvious to even the casual observer. Young wingmen being given equal rights to shoot under the tutelage of hugely experienced, patch-wearing (FWS) Eagle drivers demonstrated a mode of operation that was poles apart from that seen in the air war over Vietnam some 20 years previously. Inconceivable as it would have seemed back then, institutions like the Fighter Weapons

The F-15 community was still learning to move away from a VID mentality towards a BVR mindset when *Desert Storm* came along. (*Gary Klett via Author*)

An appropriate moniker for the flagship of the 33rd TFW, personifying the qualities necessary for success in modern air combat. The Eglin-based 33rd headed the scoreboard for aerial victories in *Desert Storm* by the close of the conflict. (*Ted Carlson*)

School and exercises like *Red Flag* had allowed F-15 squadrons to take fledgling Eagle pilots and quickly mature them into effective warriors.

Indeed, the level of skill demonstrated by the likes of Dave Sveden, Mark Arriola, Larry Pitts, Mark Williams, Bob Hehemann, and many others was key to allowing many of the kills to take place, whether that be because they had taken the initiative and were the shooter, or because they were supporting the shooter with such competence and SA that he could concentrate on his own shot. At the very least, *Desert Storm* had put the final nail in the coffin for the old saying that wingmen should be seen and not heard.

The local influences are less obvious, although the signs are there if one looks closely enough. In the first instance, location had a lot to do with the amount of 'luck' that each squadron would have when actually encountering the IrAF. Pre-war planning had worked on the basis that most Iraqi aircraft would be encountered east of Baghdad, and that the 1st TFW at Dhahran would enjoy the majority of the engagements. In fact, in the first few weeks at least, the majority of aircraft sightings were observed west of Baghdad, providing the 58th TFS at Tabuk with more opportunities to test their mettle for real.

As the war moved on, and the IrAF began to run to Iran in earnest, the Barrier CAPs flown by the Eagles from 'PSAB', Incirlik and Tabuk provided numerous kill opportunities against fuel-starved fighters as they fled east in desperation. Of course, being closest, one would have expected the 1st TFW at Dhahran to have grabbed these opportunities with both hands, but it did not. For reasons that are variously attributed to a lack of leadership, poor sortie generation rates, and an unwillingness to assume BARCAP responsibilities too far north of Baghdad, Langley's leadership declined numerous ATO taskings to provide BARCAP fighters. The Air Force's oldest fighter wing ended the war with a meagre single kill as a result.

Other local influences over individual unit kill ratios include the style of leadership and the balance between experienced and inexperienced deployed aircrew. The leadership style affected the

75

manner in which sortie scheduling was conducted – Bitburg and Eglin commanders allowed captains and majors to lead sorties and lieutenants to fly as wingmen, whereas Langley's commanders preferred to fly missions themselves, sidelining the younger warriors who would have been better suited to the task.

Throughout my research, the then 58th TFS commander – Lt Col Bill 'Tonic' Thiel – has been praised consistently for resisting the urge to out-rank his flight leads and dominate proceedings (although the desire to do so must have been strong indeed). Thiel instead flew as Nos 4 or 8 in a formation – always there with his troops, but never dominating events on the basis of rank or total flying hours.

Thiel's style of leadership created a culture in which his younger pilots could seize the opportunity to learn and grow, but most importantly he provided his experienced FWS graduates with the opportunity to apply their skill and knowledge to the air war. In contrast, the 1st TFW has been described as being 'top heavy' at the time. Indeed, it operated quite differently. For example, I was told the story of one experienced major at Dhahran who should have been flying, but was instead planning and performing flight briefings on behalf of senior leadership who had scheduled themselves on missions that they were too busy to actually give the briefings for.

Finally, the 58th TFS undoubtedly benefited from the unusually high ratio of FWS graduates amongst its ranks. It was this experience that enabled it to fly daytime formations at night, and that allowed its pilots to possess enough spare mental capacity to solve complex problems in real-time, and under the most demanding of combat conditions. Draeger, Kelk, Tollini, Magill and Graeter had all gone through the school. Mistakes were certainly made, but the corresponding lessons were learned quickly, too.

All in all, these men typified the consummate FWS professional, inspiring and leading by example. Combined with their hard-crewing practices, talented young wingmen, recent *Red Flag* experience, and sound leadership, they allowed the unit to dominate the skies over Iraq during *Desert Storm*.

In contrast to the 33rd TFW, the 1st TFW lacked the heavyweight experience at captain level that was abundant within the Eglin squadrons. This, and what some pilots who served with the unit at the time have described as overly autocratic leadership, left the 1st TFW with far fewer kills than it might otherwise have achieved. (Gary Klett via Author)

THE EAGLE AND THE 'FULCRUM'

From 1993 onwards, F-15s supported a range of NATO and UN operations in the Balkans theatre. In June 1991, the former Yugoslavia began its violent break up when the Republic of Slovenia and Croatia declared independence from the Federal Government in Belgrade. When civil war broke out in Bosnia a year later, the United Nations passed Resolution 757 introducing economic sanctions against Serbia and Montenegro.

NATO operations began in earnest when AWACS aircraft started monitoring a no-fly zone over Bosnia-Herzegovina in October 1992 under the auspices of UN Security Council Resolution 781. Operation *Deny Flight* commenced on 12 April 1993, and involved a range of UN reconnaissance and fighter aircraft, mostly based in Italy, enforcing the no-fly zone. By July, F-15Cs from Bitburg's 53rd FS had flown over 660 CAP sorties, protecting NATO troops on the ground in the Baltic regions of Banja Luca and Sarajevo.

In early 1994, USAF F-16s downed four Serbian jets as they contravened the no-fly zone. Over the course of the year, diplomatic efforts deteriorated, leading to a limited NATO strike against Serbian targets in Croatia, in particular Udbina airfield, in November 1994. The strike force of some 30 jets was protected by pairs of F-15Cs.

Operation *Deliberate Force* followed the August 1995 shelling of the market square in Sarajevo, punitive strikes hitting Serbian armour and supplies around Sarajevo on 30 August. Once again these jets were protected from the Serbian Air Force by F-15Cs. In the days that followed, similar protection was provided as more strikes were flown.

Operation *Allied Force* (OAF) followed repeated NATO warnings in 1998 to Serbian President Slobodan Milosevic to remove his armed forces from Kosovo. Fifteen F-15Cs from the 493rd FS/48th FW, based at RAF Lakenheath, England, deployed to Aviano AB, Italy, in order to provide CAP

The AIM-120 AMRAAM was introduced to the F-15 at the end of *Desert Storm*. By the time the 493rd FS deployed to Operation *Allied Force*, the standard load was a combination of AIM-7, AIM-9 and AIM-120 missiles. This 'Grim Reaper' Eagle banks away from the tanker as it returns to its *Allied Force* CAP in March 1999. (*USAF*)

support and OCA duties. NATO adopted a five-phase plan – initially, its military flights would act as a deterrent, only becoming more aggressive if NATO demands were not met.

Despite diplomatic gains made at the Rambouillet talks in France, additional NATO strike assets were still arriving in-theatre as late as February 1999, and newly arrived F-117 stealth fighters

displaced Lakenheath's Eagles from Aviano to Cervia AB. They were simultaneously reinforced to a total strength of 18 aircraft, as jets were sent directly to Italy from a seven-week Operation *Northern Watch* (see Chapter 5) deployment in Turkey.

Operation *Noble Anvil* – the name given to the US portion of OAF – kicked off on the night of 24 March 1999. The 493rd FS would claim four MiG-29s destroyed during the brief campaign.

YUGOSLAV AIR FORCE

In 1991, the Federal Republic of Yugoslavia (FRY) shrunk to less than a third of its original size following its independence – the country now comprised just Montenegro and Serbia. Following the cessation of hostilities and the subsequent Dayton Peace Accords in 1995, the FRY Air Force reduced its inventory. By 1998, it was assessed to have a mixed force of jet fighters on strength, including 60 MiG-21s, 16 MiG-29 'Fulcrums' and 60+ Orao fighter-bombers.

With the job of defending a landlocked country, the FRYAF knew that there were a limited number of routes that NATO could use to approach the country without violating the sovereign airspace of neighbouring nations. Its task was therefore simplified. Like the IrAF almost a decade before, the FRYAF too enjoyed the protection of a multi-layered and mobile IADS, much of which was located in the mountains, and was therefore very difficult for NATO to target. This SAM threat worried the F-15 community more than the FRYAF itself.

The FRY government had no illusions about the fate of its MiG-29 fleet were it to attempt to fight NATO head-on. However, it had

The 493rd FS was originally an F-111F squadron prior to it switching to the F-15C in 1994. The unit patch, which shows a bomb striking home, is a source of many good-natured jokes for the two F-15E squadrons that live alongside the 'Grim Reapers' at RAF Lakenheath! (Author/FJPhotography.com)

A 493rd FS F-15C fires an AIM-7 Sparrow missile during the annual Combat Archer air-to-air weapons evaluation at Tyndall AFB, in Florida. (Gary Klett via Author)

struggled to maintain its fleet of 'Fulcrums' even before the war, and knew that a post-war Yugoslavia could not afford to keep them flying. It therefore made a conscious decision to sacrifice its MiG-29s, whilst protecting the remainder of its air force.

MiG KILLS

At 2200 hrs local time on 24 March 1999, the 493rd FS's Capt Mike Shower (in F-15C 86-0159) became the first 'Grim Reaper' to score a kill when he fired an AIM-120 AMRAAM at a MiG-29 'Fulcrum' as it lifted off from its airfield at Batajnica. Shower initially fired two AMRAAMs without success, but the third, fired at closer range (six miles), found its target.

The second MiG-29 kill that night fell to Lt Col Cesar Rodriguez, a double MiG-killing veteran of *Desert Storm*. Rodriguez (in F-15C 86-0169) claimed his third kill while flying OCA over the war-torn city of Pristina. He was No 3 in a four-ship F-15 OCA force – 'Knife' flight, mission 4125F – assigned to protect NATO's first strike package of the war. The fighter-bombers were targeting Montenegro airfield, 'and was also going to take out the EW radars that were linking the adjoining Kosovo/Montenegro airspace. We were to open up a lane of attack to make the province of Kosovo accessible without contention', recalled Rodriguez.

'Knife' flight would lead everyone into battle – even the stealthy B-2s were scheduled to follow behind it. The mission commander was the F-16 lead pilot, Lt Col Dave Goldfein, while 'Knife' would be led by Robert 'Cricket' Renner (the 493rd FS's FWS graduate and weapons officer), with 'K-Bob' as No 2, Rodriguez No 3 and 'Wild Bill' Denim, a recently winged Eagle 'baby', as No 4.

As the C-models took off at sunset, Rodriguez noted the eerie juxtaposition between the dark abyss – and war – to the east, and the sun setting to the west, bathing Italy in a beautiful warm light as the night life started up and people ventured into restaurants and bars for meals and drinks.

Having taken on fuel and positioned some 40 to 50 miles ahead of the main strike force, Rodriguez remembered:

'We flew south along the Italian ADIZ (Air Defence Identification Zone), all the way down to "the boot" at the southern tip of Italy. Then we turned east, coming up along the eastern edge of the Adriatic. We pushed it up and began our climb to 35,000 ft, with the strike package behind us.'

Approaching the target area, Rodriguez's flight began to observe a contact which quickly landed before they could engage it.

'That aeroplane executed an instrument approach into Montenegro airfield, and the pilot witnessed first-hand the destruction of the airfield. He may even have experienced a bomb or two himself, as he probably did not make it to his hardened facility.

'As we continued to head north, "Wild Bill" and I were the easternmost element, and we were looking at the airspace between Belgrade and Kosovo. "Cricket" and "K-Bob" were looking at Montenegro. I detected a target flying out of Kosovo airfield which initially headed north and stayed at low altitude for some 15 miles. It then popped up on a southwesterly vector, putting him on a direct intercept with the strikers heading towards Montenegro. As he turned to the southwest and climbed from a couple of hundred feet, we began our initial intercept and started working with NATO AWACS for validation of its identity. We also commenced our own EID matrix.'

The MiG had been detected and locked up at 1909 hrs, flying at 6000 ft, some 40 degrees and 62 miles off of Rodriguez's nose. AWACS was unable to identify it as hostile at this stage, and two minutes later it beamed to a heading of 300 degrees, causing Rodriguez's radar to drop the lock. At the same instant, Renner ('Knife' 11) transmitted that he had an intermittent radar failure.

At 1912:25 hrs Rodriguez reacquired the target and gave 'Knife 11' a 'Bulls Eye' range/bearing reading, recommending that he focus his radar in that direction. At 1912:36 hrs he asked AWACS to declare his target, but received a 'bogey' reply, indicating that AWACS was not yet sure. Less than a second later, 'Knife 14' transmitted that NCTR indications in his cockpit indicated that the target was a MiG-29.

Still waiting to engage, and now down to 30 miles separation from the target, Rodriguez 'jettisoned the wing tanks so that we could go a little bit faster, climbed to about 33,000 ft and accelerated to Mach 1.4'. At 1913:25 hrs he fired 'a single AIM-120 against the single contact. The missile came off the rail, shot out in front of me and then selected a lead pursuit curve commensurate to a positive intercept. We executed an F-pole (at 1913:27 hrs) to the southeast so that we avoided going into the Kosovo SAM belts, and tracked the missile towards closure.

Below and right
The wreckage of the MiG-29 downed by Cesar Rodriguez on 24 March 1999 was located and examined by USAF investigators. Small flags in the ground indicate the presence of explosive ordnance or fuses. (USAF)

'Still 15 to 16 miles away, I came back to pure pursuit to assess the missile's status, and everything was going well, so I stayed on course (and waited for the timer to count down to zero). The MiG was obviously still full of gas, because as the counter hit zero (at 1914:06 hrs), there was a phenomenal explosion. If you had put several football fields together and lit them up all at the same time then that's what it looked like. The intercept happened over the western mountains of Kosovo, and they were still covered with snow – the reflection of the explosion off of the snow had the guys on the strikes well south of Montenegro wondering what the hell we had hit.'

The final two kills for the 493rd came courtesy of Capt Jeff Hwang (in F-15C 86-0156) on 26 March 1999. Hwang was tasked as the Bosnia-Herzegovina DCA flight lead on 26 March, and was to provide cover for a vulnerability time of 1500 to 1900 hrs. He and his wingman were eastbound, approaching the Bosnia/Yugoslavia border, having established their orbit over Tuzla following initial refuelling, when he picked up a radar contact 37 miles to the east at 6000 ft, beaming south at over 600 knots. The time was 1602 hrs.

Hwang called out the contact and 'Boomer' McMurray, his wingman, confirmed that he saw the same on his radar. Unable to immediately EID the contact, and with AWACS unable to see it, Hwang elected not to cross the border, but to enter a right-hand turn to run parallel with it on a southwest heading. He simultaneously called, 'Push it up! Burner! Tapes on!', to accelerate the flight from its leisurely 0.85 Mach at 28,000 ft to just below the Mach.

He continued his run for 60 seconds (ten nautical miles) before directing the formation to turn back 'hot', coming through south to east in an attempt to get some cut-off on the contact. 'Boomer' McMurray was on the north (left) side of the formation, and both he and Hwang picked up the contacts at 070 degrees, 37 miles away. Flying at 23,000 ft, the jets were now heading west, straight at them.

Hwang was convinced that the contact was a FRYAF fighter because of its location, and the fact that there were no NATO OCA missions over the border at that time. He checked for friendly IFF signals but received no reply, so he called AWACS and asked for permission to engage. AWACS failed to respond, although it had just begun to detect the west-bound contacts on its own radar. Accordingly, 'Dirk' flight continued with its own EID matrix as the contact closed to within 30 miles. The F-15 pilots classified the target as a MiG-29.

As he secured the EID, Hwang called on 'Boomer' McMurray to maintain the lock while he went back to search mode and began to sanitise the area around the contact for any trailers. The target check-turned to the northwest and descended to the 'high teens', so 'Dirk' flight checked 30 degrees left to northeast to maintain the cut-off. Having been momentarily placed behind McMurray in the left-turn, Hwang repositioned himself in line abreast, and then called for the jettisoning of the flight's wing tanks.

Now well above the Mach, Hwang positioned his radar elevation coverage to look from 5000 ft up to 21,000 ft in an effort to make one last sweep for trailers or other unseen contacts. AWACS simultaneously started calling out two contacts in a lead-trail formation – sure enough, he could see on his scope that his radar was just beginning to break out a second fighter in very close formation with the first. With the distance closed to some 20 miles, and the contacts at 18,000 ft, McMurray called, 'Fox 3' as he unleashed an AIM-120 AMRAAM.

Hwang locked up the leader at about 17 nautical miles, immediately thumbed forward to his High Data TWS (HDTWS) mode and then shot his own AIM-120 inside of 16 miles. He then stepped his acquisition cursors to the trailing 'Fulcrum' and held the pickle button down to command a second AIM-120 on its way. Hwang was about to score the F-15's first ever multi-bogey, double MiG kill.

Assuming that McMurray had locked the leader, Hwang kept the trailer as his primary designated target. He stayed in HDTWS as the slant range closed to less than ten miles. Both targets started a check-turn to the southwest, and continued to descend into the 'low teens'. 'Dirk flight' checked their RWRs to make sure that they were not

Jeff Hwang's jet (86-0156) was marked with two Serbian kill symbols (denoting his exploits over Tuzla on 26 March 1999) until they were deleted in late 2002. (*Author/FJPhotography.com*)

The 493rd FS switched from the F-111F to the F-15C in 1992. Since then it has been in the thick of the action, and it is the only Eagle unit to have scored kills since *Desert Storm*. (*Gary Klett via Author*)

being targeted, and then pointed their noses at the MiGs, assuming a pure pursuit curve. They rolled inverted from 30,000 ft and pointed their noses low and directly at the TD box in their HUDs.

Pulling the throttles to idle, Hwang saw a tiny dot in the TD box about seven to eight miles out against a broken cloud background. He called, 'Dirk 1, Tally-Ho, Nose, seven miles, low!' Realising it was the trailer, he waited for McMurray to call that he had the leader in sight. Approaching five miles, and with no call from McMurray, he scanned without success in front of the trailer for the leader.

The trailer continued its left turn to the southwest, and Hwang thumbed aft to AIM-9 and tried twice to uncage a missile, only to discover that there was no missile tone. At that instant, between his HUD and canopy bow, he saw the leader explode spectacularly at his 'one o'clock' position. Turning his attention back to the trailer, it too exploded into a streaking ball of flame seconds later.

Hwang called for McMurray to assume a 080-degree heading and run his short-range radar. He thumbed aft to Auto Guns and plugged in full afterburner to accelerate to 460 knots and climb back to 20,000 ft. 'Dirk 2' then called, 'Blind!', but 'Dirk 1' quickly located him visually three miles north (left) and stacked high. Waiting a few moments to check one last time for more hostile fighters to the east, Hwang and McMurray turned to the west and departed the area.

Hwang had flown a well-executed intercept according to basic USAF doctrine – manoeuvre for displacement, check EID, shoot, F-pole, and displace again, *or* go pure pursuit if target falls within ten miles, enter BFM if required. His decision to follow his AIM-120s to the target instead of F-poling was influenced by two factors. Firstly, he was winning the fight – at least he was not being fired upon – and secondly, he had closed to within ten miles of his foe, which was the F-15's unwritten range after which it should no longer turn and run.

It was later determined that McMurray's AIM-120 had failed to hit its target. Hwang's near simultaneous multi-bogey AIM-120 engagement had brought down both 'Fulcrums'.

CHANGING TIMES

In much the same way as technology and weapons systems had evolved and influenced tactics between Rob Graeter's early years in the 1980s at Kadena, and his experiences almost a decade later in the Saudi desert, so too had things changed between Cesar Rodriguez's first two victories in 1991 and his third kill in 1999.

The AIM-120 AMRAAM had superseded the AIM-7M Sparrow in late 1991 (in fact, Chuck Magill had flown the first operational F-15 AMRAAM sortie at the end of *Desert Storm*), paving the way for new tactics to be developed. AMRAAM required the shooter to support it until its own on-board active seeker had acquired the target, at which point the shooter was free to leave the area. It used a secure data link with the launch aircraft to report its position, allowing accurate fly-out indications to be displayed in the shooter's cockpit, This in turn meant that the F-15 pilot knew where the missile was relative to the target.

But AMRAAM requires a good radar to support it, so the APG-63's constant development and investment is equally as important as the

emergence of the missile itself. Indeed, Hwang was able to engage two targets simultaneously from TWS mode only because the APG-70 in the nose of his fighter was good enough to accomplish such a feat – a capability that pilots could only have dreamed of during ODS.

For all of those advancements, the core on-board EID capability was almost certainly the key ingredient once again in all four engagements, particularly Hwang's double kill. The performance of the NATO AWACS in OAF, both in human and technological terms, has been heavily criticised. AWACS controllers consistently underperformed, failing to provide timely clearances and advisories when the Eagles needed them most. Hwang's experience is a case in point – he later said that he was sure that he did not get a response from AWACS to his coded request for permission to engage simply because the controller was unfamiliar with the code word that he used.

Rodriguez also observed that some AWACS crews underperformed by a significant margin,

This dramatic photograph shows the launching of an AIM-120 AMRAAM from an F-15D. The weapon has rapidly climbed to altitude after being fired, at which point it starts contrailing. Ultimately, it will impact a Firebee target drone. (*Gary Klett via Author*)

and this did little to inspire the confidence of the OCA and DCA 'cappers'. He said of the NATO AWACS controllers, 'they were ill-prepared or ill-trained to meet their role in the ID matrix'.

Some things had remained unchanged over the years, however. Of particular interest is that the formation flown by the 493rd FS in their night sorties was similar to the off-set trail that Graeter had opted for on the first night of *Desert Storm*.

Some F-15 squadrons had night vision goggles by 1999, but the 'Grim Reapers' had yet to receive them – they therefore elected to fly the tried and tested 'defence in depth' formation. This allowed the supporting two-ship element flying 25 miles in trail to kill the target if the first element was unable to do so itself.

In such a scenario, the first element would disengage and flow in behind the second element in what resembled an airborne wagon wheel. Like off-set trail, defence in depth not only alleviated the second element's position-keeping workload by making use of the radar to help keep correct spacing, but also permitted the Nos 2 and 4 to trail some three to five miles behind Nos 1 and 3.

BLUE ON BLUE

On 14 April 1994, tragedy struck when the 26 crew and passengers of two US Army UH-60 Blackhawk helicopters were downed over northern Iraq by two F-15Cs flown by Capt Eric Wickson (lead) and Lt Col Randy W May (wingman) – May already had the contentious Mi-24 kill to his credit from three years previously, and was now the CO of the 53rd FS. The Air Force attributed the incident to a chain of errors, from the general heading up the Operation *Provide Comfort* Task Force all the way down.

The day started at 0635 hrs with the launch of two F-15Cs – 'Tiger 01' and '02' – on a sweep of the airspace north of the no-fly zone, then transitioning into a DCA/CAP mission in the area. At 0654 hrs the two UH-60s took off from Zakhu using the 'Eagle' call-sign, and informed AWACS (call sign 'Cougar') of their departure point and their destination. At 0720 hrs Wickson, in 'Tiger 01', reported entering northern Iraq to 'Cougar', and then went about leading his flight on a sweep of the area in search of Iraqi aircraft.

Since the ATO did not contain any detailed information about the 'Eagle' flight, the AWACS controller did not pass the relevant information to the F-15 pilots, who had no idea that a friendly helicopter flight was operating in the very same airspace it was assigned to 'delouse'.

Two minutes later, Wickson reported a radar contact on a low-flying, slow-moving aircraft approximately 52 miles north of the southern boundary of the no-fly zone, and 40 miles southeast of his own position. 'Cougar' responded with a 'clean there' call, meaning that the controller aboard the AWACS had no targets on his

Two 53rd FS/36th FW F-15Cs identical to this one were involved in the 14 April 1994 'Blue on Blue' incident which resulted in the destruction of two US Army UH-60s and 26 military personnel in northern Iraq. This particular jet was transferred from the 36th to the 325th FTW just months prior to the shoot-down. (*Bob Archer*)

A US Army UH-60 similar to the two Blackhawks downed in the friendly fire incident in April 1994. (*US Army*)

85

scope. The F-15 pilots plotted an intercept to investigate, while using IFF to probe the contacts for a friendly electronic response.

The gap had closed to 20 miles by 0725 hrs (some three minutes after 'Tiger 01' had detected the radar contacts), when Wickson once again called the contacts out to 'Cougar', who responded this time with 'hits there', indicating that he too saw the radar contact. In fact 'Cougar' was receiving the IFF returns from 'Eagle' flight's IFF transponders – the AWACS was not actually detecting them via direct radar returns.

A minute later, the IFF returns from the UH-60 was not only clearly visible, but also identifiable as being in the same location as Wickson's reported contacts, yet AWACS still did not inform the 'Tiger' flight of the presence of IFF data in the target area. Wickson locked the target up and then initiated his own IFF interrogations in both commercial and military (Mode IV) modes, each six-second-long attempt failed to illicit a response. 'Tiger 01' and '02' moved in closer to make a visual identification.

At 0727 hrs, Wickson closed to seven miles and visually identified the contact as a helicopter, calling '"Tiger 01" is tally, one helicopter. Standby VID'. He passed 'Eagle 01' at a height of 500 ft, 1000 ft to the left at 450 knots (giving an overtake of 320 knots – 'Eagle' was at 130 knots), then pulled off high and to the right over the top of the helicopter so as to avoid any forward-firing armament that an adversary gunship might have. He observed that the helicopter was carrying sponsons fitted with ordnance, but was otherwise unable to see any distinguishing markings on the camouflaged green helicopter.

He radioed, '"Tiger 01". VID "Hind" – no, "Hip"', at 0728 hrs, before referring to an in-flight silhouette guide to clarify his VID. Wickson then called, '"Tiger 01", disregard "Hip". VID "Hind"'. With that he reversed course from the southeast to the northwest, before acquiring a visual on the second helicopter, trailing 'Eagle 01' by two miles. His call '"Tiger 01". VID "Hind", tally two, lead-trail', prompted 'Cougar' to respond, 'Copy "Hinds"'. Wickson now sought confirmation of his VID from May in 'Tiger 02'. '"Tiger 02", confirm "Hinds"'. He later reported receiving the response, 'Standby'.

It is at this point that the final series of errors occurred – May flew 2000 ft to the right of the trailing helicopter and transmitted, '"Tiger 02", tally two' to say that he had both helicopters in sight. This transmission, though, was interpreted by Wickson to mean that May had concurred with his 'Hind' VID, whereas May simply meant to state that he had the two helicopters in sight.

Wickson then told AWACS, '"Cougar", "Tiger 02" has tallied two "Hinds", engaged', and then

The F-15 pilots thought they were attacking a Mi-24 gunship identical to this one. Indeed, the leader of 'Tiger' flight went as far as to positively identify the helicopter as a 'Hind'. (*USAF*)

flew to a point ten miles to the helicopters' northwest in a pre-arranged move that allowed the F-15 pilots time to make a perfect attack.

As he rolled back towards the helicopters, Wickson called, '"Tiger" arm hot, "Tiger 01" is hot', telling May that he was cleared to fire provided that ROE were met. He then transmitted on the AUX radio, 'We're coming up behind them. There's two in lead-trail. "Tiger 01" is going first. I will shoot the trailer and then you will shoot the leader'. Wickson and May switched to AUTO ACQ mode to acquire their quarry and then attempted a final IFF interrogation, before visually acquiring their respective targets in their HUDs.

'"TIGER 01", fox. "TIGER 01", splash one "Hind". "Tiger 02", you're engaged with the second one. He's off my nose two miles, right past the fireball. "02" call in. "01's" off left'. Wickson had despatched the trailing UH-60 with an AIM-120 fired from about four miles out. May followed with an AIM-9 fired about 9000 ft away from 'Eagle 01'. '"Tiger 02" in hot. "Tiger 02", splash second "Hind"'. May reportedly ended the engagement with the words, 'Stick a fork in him – he's done!'

END OF AN ERA

In March 2003, a US, British, and Australian military force entered Iraq and removed Saddam Hussein from power. The liberation of Iraq brought to an end Operations *Southern* and *Northern Watch*, and Britain and America quietly removed all of their forces from Turkey, and left only a skeleton staff in Saudi Arabia.

With concerns over safety, and diplomatic tensions running high between Saudi Arabia and its former protectors, future military operations against the remnants of Saddam's regime are likely to be based in Kuwait, Qatar, or Iraq itself. Operation *Iraqi Freedom*, as the campaign in Iraq is known, has closed the door on a remarkable era.

Its tanks topped off, a fully armed 33rd FW F-15C peels away from the tanker somewhere over southern Iraq in early 2003. (*USAF*)

APPENDICES

USAF & RSAF F-15C EAGLE KILL LISTS

USAF

Date	F-15	Pilot	Unit	Weapon	Kill
17/1/91	85-0125	Capt John Kelk	58th TFS	AIM-7M	MiG-29
17/1/91	85-0105	Capt Robert E Graeter	58th TFS	AIM-7M	2 x Mirage F 1EQ
17/1/91	85-0119	Capt Rhory Draeger* (59th TFS)	58th TFS	AIM-7M	MiG-29
17/1/91	85-0107	Capt Charles Magill (USMC)**	58th TFS	AIM-7M	MiG-29
17/1/91	83-0017	Capt Steve Tate	71st TFS	AIM-7M	Mirage F 1EQ
19/1/91	85-0099	Capt Larry Pitts	58th TFS	AIM-7M	MiG-25
19/1/91	85-0101	Capt Richard C Tollini	58th TFS	AIM-7M	MiG-25
19/1/91	85-0122	Capt Craig Underhill**	58th TFS	AIM-7M	MiG-29
19/1/91	85-0114	Capt Cesar A Rodriguez Jr	58th TFS	Hit Ground	MiG-29
19/1/91	79-0021	Lt David G Sveden (22nd TFS)	525th TFS	AIM-7M	Mirage F 1EQ
19/1/91	79-0069	Capt David S Prather	525th TFS	AIM-7M	Mirage F 1EQ
26/1/91	85-0104	Capt Anthony Schiavi	58th TFS	AIM-7M	MiG-23
26/1/91	85-0108	Capt Rhory Draeger (59th TFS)	58th TFS	AIM-7M	MiG-23
26/1/91	85-0114	Capt Cesar A Rodriguez Jr	58th TFS	AIM-7M	MiG-23
27/1/91	84-0025	Capt Jay T Denney	53rd TFS	AIM-9M	2 x MiG-23
27/1/91	84-0027	Capt Benjamin D Powell	53rd TFS	AIM-7M	MiG-23 & Mirage F 1EQ
28/1/91	79-0022	Capt Donald S Watrous	32nd TFS	AIM-7M	MiG-23
29/1/91	85-0102	Capt David Rose (60th TFS)	58th TFS	AIM-7M	MiG-23
2/2/91	79-0064	Capt Gregory Masters	525th TFS	AIM-7M	Il-76
6/2/91	79-0078	Capt Thomas N Dietz	53rd TFS	AIM-9M	2 x MiG-21
6/2/91	84-0019	Lt Robert W Hehemann	53rd TFS	AIM-9M	2 x Su-25
7/2/91	85-0102	Capt Anthony R Murphy	58th TFS	AIM-7M	2 x Su-22
7/2/91	84-0124	Col Rick Parsons	58th TFS	AIM-7M	1 x Su-7
7/2/91	80-0003	Ma. Randy May	525th TFS	AIM-7M	Mi-24
11/2/91	79-0048	Capt Steven Dingy	525th TFS	AIM-7M	0.5 Mi-8
11/2/91	80-0012	Capt Mark Mckenzie	525th TFS	AIM-7M	0.5 Mi-8***
20/3/91	84-0014	Capt John Doneski	53rd TFS	AIM-7M	Su-22
22/3/91	84-0010	Capt Thomas N Dietz	53rd TFS	AIM-9M	Su-22
22/3/91	84-0015	Lt Robert W Hehemann	53rd TFS	Hit Ground	PC-9
24/3/99	86-0159	Capt Mike Shower	493rd FS	AIM-120	MiG-29
24/3/99	86-0169****	Lt Col Cesar A Rodriguez Jr	493rd FS	AIM-120	MiG-29
26/3/99	86-0156	Capt Jeff Hwang	493rd FS	AIM-120	2 x MiG-29

RSAF

Date	F-15	Pilot	Unit	Weapon	Kill
5/6/84	?	?	?	AIM-7	Iranian F-4E
24/1/91	80-0068	Saleh Al-Shamrani	No 13 Sqn	AIM-9M	2 x Mirage F 1EQ

Notes

* Draeger died in a car accident in 1995.

** It is believed either Magill or Underhill shot down the MiG-29 flown by IrAF Col Walid, a former MiG-21 and Mirage F 1EQ pilot. He ejected safely and was shepherded to Saudi Arabia by Bedouin who had witnessed the engagement. There he sought, and was granted, political asylum.

*** According to the USAF Historical Research Agency, the identity of this helicopter differs from one report to another.

**** This airframe was subsequently lost on 26 March 2001 following a fatal crash over Scotland.

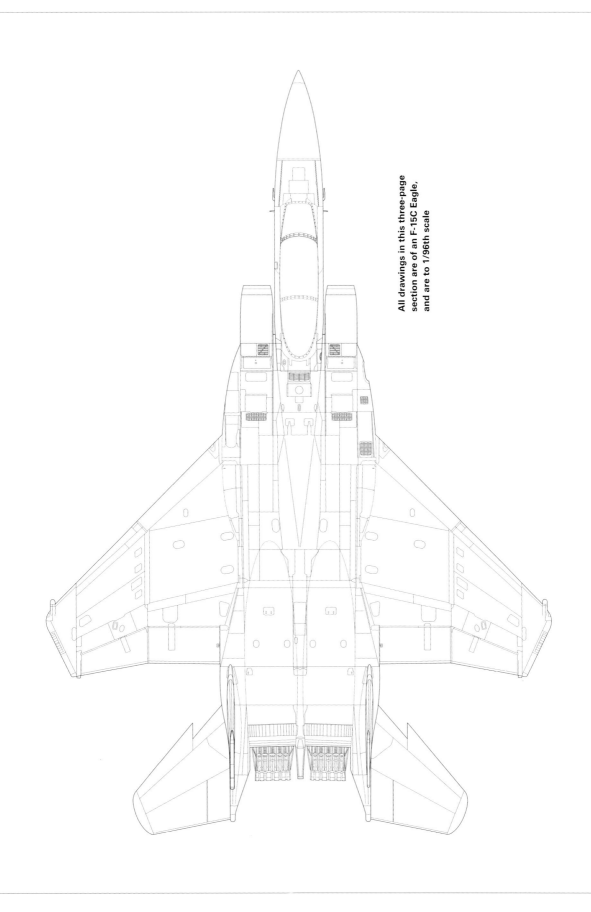

All drawings in this three-page section are of an F-15C Eagle, and are to 1/96th scale

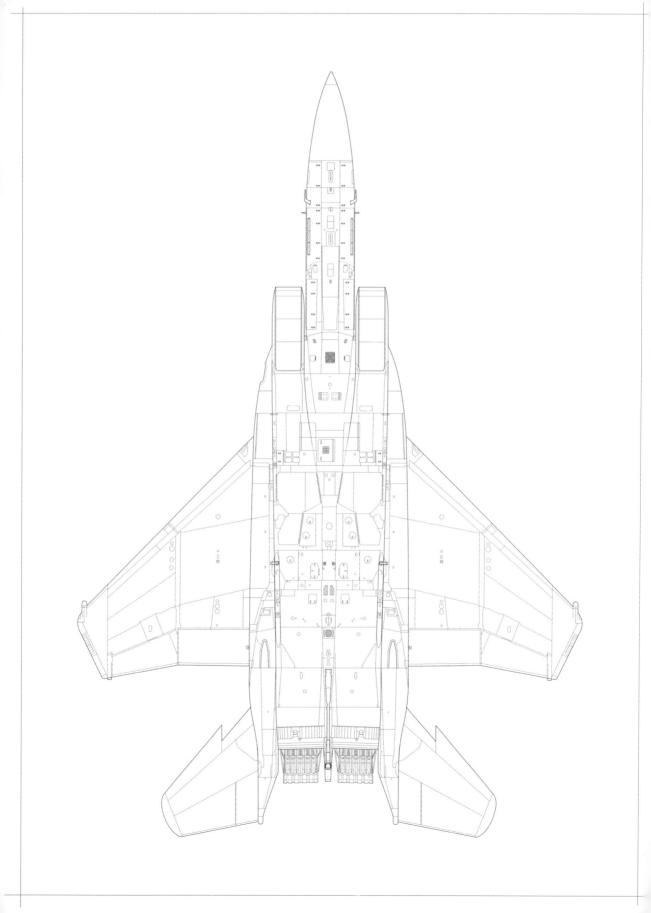

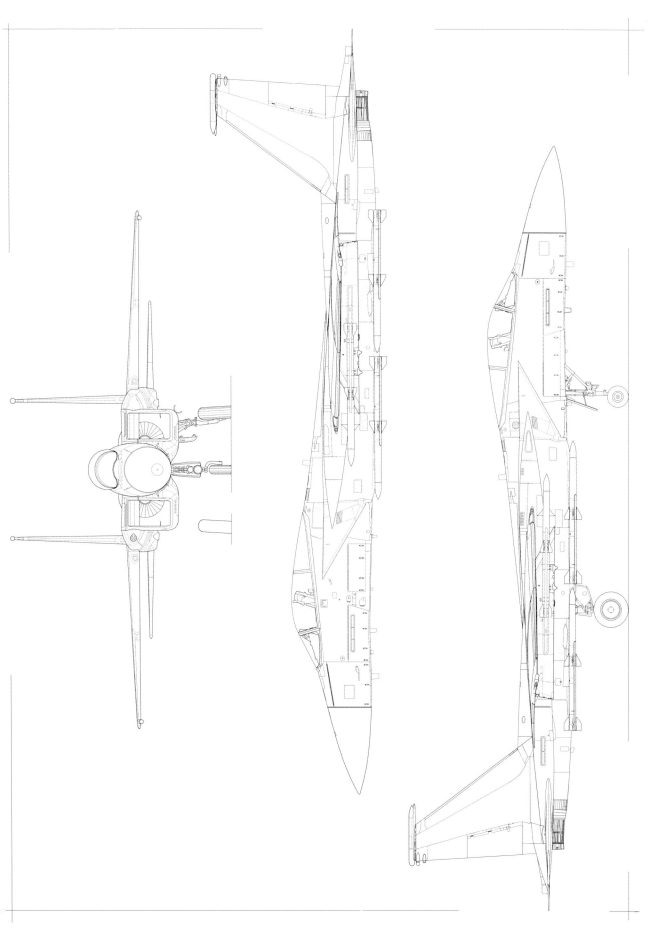

COLOUR PLATES

1

F-15C 605 of No 13 Sqn, Dhahran AB, Saudi Arabia, late 1990

The Royal Saudi Air Force took delivery of 56 F-15Cs in two lots of 47 and nine. The RSAF serial numbers of these airframes are difficult to match to the original McDonnell Douglas serial numbers because the Saudis use their own discrete tail codes. An additional 24 F-15C/Ds were hastily supplied to the RSAF by the US government from USAFE stocks in September–October 1990.

2

F-15C 1309 of No 13 Sqn, Dhahran AB, Saudi Arabia, late 1990

The RSAF scored its first Eagle kills when two F-15s on a refuelling exercise attacked a pair of Iranian F-4E Phantom IIs in 1984. One aircraft was damaged, but managed to make an emergency landing, and the other was destroyed with the loss of both crew. The second and third kills at the hands of the Saudi Eagles came during the *Desert Storm*, when a lone F-15C intercepted and despatched two IrAF Mirage F 1EQs with AIM-9 Sidewinders. The victorious aircraft came from No 13 Sqn.

3

F-15C 84-0019 of the 53rd TFS/36th TFW, Bitburg AB, Germany, mid-1991

F-15C-38-MC 84-0019 was used by Lt Bob Hehemann to down two IrAF Su-25 'Frogfoots' attempting to flee to Iran on 6 February 1991. It is depicted here in artwork replete with the two kill markings applied shortly after the return of the squadron to Bitburg AB, in Germany. The airframe remained at Bitburg until 1994, when the squadron moved to nearby Spangdahlem AB. In 1999 it was one of six Eagles to be transferred to the 493rd FS/48th FW at RAF Lakenheath, in England, when the 53rd FS was deactivated. 84-0019 continues to serve with the 493rd FS today, and also retains its kill markings. Bob Hehemann has since left the USAF and is now an airliner pilot.

4

F-15C 79-0048 of the 525th TFS(P), Incirlik AB, Turkey, February 1991

Capt Steve Dingy was flying F-15C-25-MC 79-0048 on 11 February 1991 when he fired upon – and destroyed – a helicopter. Claiming a joint kill with his flight lead that day, Capt Mark McKenzie, there has since been much confusion over the exact identity of the helicopter. Most sources report it as being a Mi-8 'Hip'. 79-0048 was one of only a handful of Block 25 machines that were not passed directly to the Royal Saudi Air Force soon after *Desert Shield* commenced in August 1990. The aircraft was based at Incirlik AB, Turkey, for the duration of the conflict, before returning home to Bitburg in mid-1991. Delivered new to the 36th TFW in December 1980, the jet spent time with both the 525th and the 53rd TFSs, before being passed on to the 3rd Wing's 54th FS at Elmendorf AFB in July 1992. Exactly two years later the aircraft was transferred to the Tyndall-based 1st FS/325th FTW, where it presently remains.

5

F-15C 85-0099 of the 58th TFS/33rd TFW, Tabuk AB, Saudi Arabia, March 1991

Adorned with a single kill marking for the destruction of a MiG-25 'Foxbat' over Iraq on 19 January 1991, F-15C-39-MC 85-0099 was being flown by Capt Larry Pitts at the time of the engagement. Wearing standard Eglin AFB tail codes and 'Gorilla' squadron markings, it is depicted here after the war as the personal jet of Capt Pitts. Standard practice when applying kill markings was to adorn the jet with one victory symbol to denote that it was used to score a kill, and to stencil a separate marking inside the name plate below the canopy sill to denote that the victory was credited to that particular pilot (irrespective of whether the airframe currently assigned to him was the same as the one in which he had scored his kill). In this particular instance, the 58th TFS deliberately assigned Pitts the jet in which he had scored his kill. 85-0099 had been delivered new to the 33rd TFW on 26 August 1986, and it served variously with the 58th and 60th TFSs until 10 January 1997, when it caught fire on take-off from Eglin. The 58th FS pilot hastily landed the jet and managed to escape uninjured once it had come to a halt, but the base fire crew could not prevent the Eagle from being completely burnt out.

6

F-15C 85-0108 of the 58th TFS/33rd TFW, Tabuk AB, Saudi Arabia, March 1991

GULF SPIRIT – aka F-15C-40-MC 85-0108 – was one of the most photographed airframes to return to Eglin AFB when the 33rd TFW came home after *Desert Storm*. It was used by Capt Rhory Draeger to destroy a MiG-23 'Flogger' with an AIM-7 Sparrow missile on 26 January 1991. The jet was one of three squadron flagships to wear the 33rd TFW tail flashes and all three squadron badges throughout the war. 85-0108 was delivered new to the 33rd on 10 December 1986, and it remained with the unit until transferred to the 3rd Wing's 54th FS in June 1998. The aircraft currently serves with the 3rd Wing's 12th FS, and it was involved in an accident at Tinker AFB, Oklahoma, on 1 February 2003 when its left main gear leg collapsed on landing. Now repaired, it is back on strength with the 12th FS.

7

F-15C 85-0114 of the 58th TFS/33rd TFW, Tabuk AB, Saudi Arabia, March 1991

The personal aircraft of Capt Cesar Rodriguez during *Desert Storm*, 85-0114 was another Block 40 Eagle (F-15C-40-MC) belonging to the 'Gorillas'. Used during the engagement and subsequent downing of a MiG-29 'Fulcrum' and MiG-23 'Flogger' on 19 and 26 January 1991, respectively, the jet bears two kill markings to denote its own success, whilst the name plate denotes the two kills assigned to Capt Rodriguez. The latter is still flying the F-15C at the time of writing. 85-0114 was delivered new to the 33rd TFW on 26 February 1987, and was flown by the group until transferred to the 3rd Wing's 19th FS in November 1998. It remains based at Elmendorf today.

8

F-15C 85-0122 of the 58th TFS/33rd TFW, Tabuk AB, Saudi Arabia, February 1991

This 58th TFS 'Gorillas' F-15C-40-MC was used by Capt Craig Underhill to down a MiG-29 'Fulcrum' on 19 January 1991. During *Desert Storm*, it wore the squadron's blue fin flash and the unit badge on its left intake nacelle. The EG tail codes identified it as an Eglin-based jet, although the unit of course operated from Tabuk AB, Saudi Arabia, for the duration of the conflict. 85-0122 assumed the identity of 'Citgo 12' on the day of the kill. Delivered to the 33rd TFW on 24 March 1987, this aircraft was transferred to the 3rd Wing in October 1998 following a four-month overhaul in the Warner Robins Air Logistics Center. It still serves with the Elmendorf-based wing. Craig Underhill remains on active duty today, most recently commanding *Red Flag* at Nellis AFB, Nevada.

9

F-15C 83-0017 of the 71st TFS/1st TFW(P), Dhahran AB, Saudi Arabia, January 1991

Capt Steve Tate was widely reported as having scored the first kill of *Desert Storm* on 17 January 1991 when he downed a MiG-29 'Fulcrum' in F-15C-35-MC Eagle 83-0017. This urban myth was started by an overly zealous CNN news crew who greeted Tate upon his return. In actual fact, Tate was the fifth MiG killer of the war, and the 1st TFW's sole MiG killing pilot. Crews in other squadrons soon began to mock CNN with the maxim, 'Better to get it first than to get it right!' The FF tail codes and red fin flash identify 83-0017 as belonging to the Langley-based 71st TFS. Originally delivered new to the 33rd TFW's 58th TFS on 1 August 1984, this aircraft transferred to the 1st TFW's 71st TFS in October 1987, and is still serving with the unit today.

10

F-15C 85-0107 of the 58th TFS/33rd TFW, Tabuk AB, Saudi Arabia, March 1991

The 58th TFS was the highest-scoring unit to return from Operation *Desert Storm*, boasting some 16 IrAF kills to its credit. Yet another Block 40 airframe, 85-0107 was used by US Marine Corps F/A-18 exchange pilot Capt Chuck Magill to score the squadron's fourth kill (and the fourth victory of the war) against the much-vaunted MiG-29 'Fulcrum' on 17 January 1991 – Day 1 of *Desert Storm*. Magill returned to the Marines after the war, and continues to serve in the USMC Reserve today. 85-0107 was delivered new to the 33rd TFW on 21 November 1986, and served exclusively with the 58th TFS until transferred to the 3rd Wing's 54th FS in July 1998. It presently flies with the 3rd's 19th FS.

11

F-15C 85-0101 of the 58th TFS/33rd TFW, Tabuk AB, Saudi Arabia, January 1991

85-0101 is a Block 39 Eagle, and it is depicted here in artwork soon after being marked with a single victory symbol. This denoted the aircraft's involvement in the destruction of a MiG-25 on 19 January 1991 by its pilot, Capt Richard Tollini, who downed the 'Foxbat' with an AIM-7 Sparrow. The load represented in this profile – three fuel tanks, four AIM-7 Sparrows and four AIM-9 Sidewinders – was typical of the load-outs used by F-15Cs in *Desert Storm*. Tollini flew the F-15 for many years after the war before recently retiring and taking up a civilian position within the USAF. Like many of the 33rd TFW's MiG killers, 85-0101 was delivered new to the wing in October 1986 and served at Eglin until transferred to the 3rd Wing in August 1998. It is currently on strength with the wing's 12th FS.

12

F-15C 86-0165 of the 58th TFS/33rd TFW, Tabuk AB, Saudi Arabia, March 1991

This Block 42 F-15C was not involved in scoring any kills during *Desert Storm*, but it does, however, bear the name of the only wing commander to be awarded a kill during the conflict. Col Rick Parsons claimed a Su-7 on 7 February 1991 when he and Capt Tony Murphy encountered a mixed flight of Iraqi fighters heading for Iran. Murphy later claimed two Su-22 'Fitters' destroyed, but rumours persist to this day that he was actually responsible for all three kills. The final F-15C to be delivered to the USAF (on 10 October 1989), 86-0165 served with the 33rd TFW's 60th and 59th TFSs until it was transferred to the 48th FW's 493rd FS at RAF Lakenheath in March 1994. The jet still flies from the Suffolk base today.

13

F-15C 85-0102 of the 58th TFS/33rd TFW, Tabuk AB, Saudi Arabia, March 1991

The aircraft flown by Capt Tony Murphy during the 7 February 1991 engagement detailed in the commentary for plate 13, F-15C-39-MC 85-0102 was responsible for the destruction of at least three IrAF aircraft during *Desert Storm*. Its first kill occurred on 29 January 1991, when Capt David Rose destroyed a MiG-23 with an AIM-7 missile. The second and third kills came via Murphy on 7 February. Delivered to the 33rd TFW in October 1986, the airframe continues to be operated by the wing from Eglin AFB.

14

F-15C 85-0104 of the 58th TFS/33rd TFW, Tabuk AB, Saudi Arabia, January 1991

Capt Tony Schiavi was flying this aircraft on 26 January 1991 when he engaged and destroyed an Iraqi MiG-23 'Flogger'. Operating out of Tabuk AB, this airframe is depicted in the markings it wore during the war. The victory symbol has yet to be applied to the airframe, although the embossed EG tail codes that were a feature of all Eglin jets pre-war have not yet been deleted in an effort to make the aircraft less conspicuous. Blanket application of 'colourful' tail codes ceased soon after 1992, when Tactical Air Command was consolidated with Strategic Air Command to become Air Combat Command. Tony Schiavi is still presently flying F-15s. Delivered to the USAF on 24 October 1986, this aircraft served with the 33rd TFW until passed on to the 3rd Wing's 19th FS in July 1998. The jet still remains operational with the unit at Elmendorf today

15

F-15C 79-0078 of the 53rd TFS/36th TFW, Bitburg AB, Germany, summer 1991

Although at least three Block 26 F-15Cs were transferred from USAFE control to the RSAF at the start of *Desert Shield*, 79-0078 was not one of them. It subsequently distinguished itself on 6 February 1991 as when Capt Tom Dietz used it to down two IrAF MiG-21s attempting to reach Iran – The aircraft is seen here in the post-*Desert Storm* 'Mod Eagle' camouflage scheme applied to all F-15 fighters shortly after the war. Dietz is currently an Active Duty F-15 pilot on secondment to the USAF Reserve. Following 13 years of service with the 36th TFW, 79-0078 transferred to the 3rd Wing's 54th FS in August 1994. It remained in Alaska until passed on to the 58th FS/33rd FW at Eglin in October 1998, and the fighter is still in service with the unit today.

16

F-15C 84-0015 of the 53rd TFS/36th TFW, Bitburg AB, Germany, summer 1991

On 22 March 1991, Lt Bob Hehemann claimed his third kill of *Desert Storm* at the controls of this F-15C-37-MC in what turned out to be one of the most compelling engagements of the entire war. He and Capt Tom Dietz engaged a PC-9 and a Su-22 which were working together to attack Kurdish refugees in northern Iraq. Dietz despatched the 'Fitter', but Hehemann was constrained by rules of engagement that prevented him from shooting the turboprop PC-9 down. Fortunately, the pilot of the latter, who was marking targets for his colleague in the Su-22 with smoke rockets, saw Hehemann roll in behind him. Fearing for his life, the Iraqi ejected from the PC-9, narrowly missing the trailing Eagle. This was the last aerial engagement of the war, occurring on 22nd March 1991. Depicted here in the post-*Desert Storm* 'Mod Eagle' camouflage scheme, 84-0015 was delivered to the USAF on 13 November 1985

and issued to the 33rd TFW. In March 1987, the aircraft was passed on to the 36th TFW's 53rd TFS, and it remained with this unit until October 1998 (by which time the 53rd was part of the 52nd FW at Spangdahlem). The F-15 was then assigned to the 493rd FS/48th FW at RAF Lakenheath, where it is still based today.

17

F-15C 84-0027 of the 53rd TFS/14th AD(P), Prince Sultan AB, Saudi Arabia, February 1991

F-15C-38-MC 84-0027 was used by Capt Benjamin Powell on 27 January 1991 to claim a Mirage F 1EQ and a MiG-23 'Flogger' destroyed with two AIM-7 Sparrow radar-guided missiles. This was the second double kill achieved by a Bitburg pilot in *Desert Storm*, the first having been scored moments earlier in the same engagement by Capt Jay T Denney when he claimed two MiG-23s in F-15C 84-0025. Having flown with the 33rd TFW from August 1986 until being transferred to the 36th TFW in December 1988, this aircraft served briefly with the 52nd FW in 1998, before seeing service with the Langley-based 94th FS/1st FW in 1999–2000. 84-0027 returned to USAFE control in October 2001 when it was assigned to the 493rd FS. It is still presently based at RAF Lakenheath.

18

F-15C 79-0021 of the 525th TFS(P)/36th TFW, Incirlik AB, Turkey, January 1991

Lt David Sveden used this aircraft to down a Mirage F 1EQ on 19 January 1991, 79-0021 being 'on loan' to the 525th TFS(P) from the 32nd TFS at Soesterberg AB. When the fighting came to an end in March, the jet was returned to the Dutch-based unit. To confuse things still further, Sveden rejoined the 36th TFW's 22nd TFS post-war, having only been seconded to the 525th for the duration of the war! David Sveden continued to fly the F-15 following *Desert Storm*, but he has now left the USAF. Delivered new to the 32nd TFS in July 1980, 79-0021 joined the 57th FS, based at Naval Air Station Keflavik, Iceland, in December 1992. The aircraft was transferred to the 325th FTW's 2nd FS in April 1995, and it is still currently assigned to this unit.

19

F-15C 85-0125 of the 58th TFS/33rd TFW, Tabuk AB, Saudi Arabia, January 1991

On the night of the 17 January 1991, Capt Jon Kelk became the first American to score an air-to-air victory in the F-15. Flying 85-0125 as 'Pennzoil 63', he engaged a MiG-29 whilst manoeuvring defensively against a radar lock from that same opponent. In the moments that followed, confusion reigned as the Eagle threw at him a series of warnings and erroneous cockpit indications. Despite these distractions, he stayed true to his instincts and training, resulting in the first kill of the war. Kelk continues to fly the F-15C with the ANG at time of writing, while 85-0125 is presently assigned to the 3rd Wing's 19th FS.

20
F-15C 85-0119 of the 58th FS/33rd FW, Eglin AFB, January 1998

Seen in the post-war markings of the 33rd FW at Eglin AFB, 85-0119 is currently serving with the 3rd Wing's 19th FS. Flown on the opening night of *Desert Storm* by Capt Rhory Draeger (seconded to the 58th TFS by its sister-squadron, the 59th TFS), the aircraft is credited with downing a single MiG-29. Of note are the new ECM antenna fairings above and below the nose (just in front of the forward canopy glass) and the angled UHF antenna also below the nose. Eagle kill markings vary from unit to unit, and the 33rd FW has adopted a system of green stars below the canopy sill. These symbols contain details of the aircraft type destroyed and when it was downed, stencilled in white.

21
F-15C 86-0156 of the 493rd FS/48th FW, Cervia AB, Italy, March 1999

On 26 March 1999, Capt Jeff Hwang became the first American pilot to engage, fire upon and down two aircraft simultaneously. It was whilst operating from Cervia AB, Italy, as part of Operation *Allied Force* that Hwang destroyed the FRYAF MiG-29s with two AIM-120B AMRAAMs. An ex-33rd TFW jet, 86-0156 remains in service with the 493rd FS at RAF Lakenheath at the time of writing, but no longer bears the two FRY flags below its canopy sill – these were erased when the Eagle was repainted in late 2003.

22
F-15C 84-0010 of the 53rd TFS/36th TFW, Bitburg AB, Germany, summer 1991

F-15C-38-MC 84-0010 was the machine piloted by Capt Thomas Dietz for his third, and final, kill against the IrAF on 22 March 1991. Rolling in behind a Su-22 'Fitter' as it dropped its ordnance on fleeing Kurdish refugees below, Dietz unleashed an AIM-9 Sidewinder missile from close-range and blew the jet out of the sky. Delivered new to the 33rd TFW in September 1985, this aircraft was passed on to the 36th TFW in January 1988. It then served with the 52nd FW from February 1994 through to December 1998, when the jet joined its current unit, the 493rd FS.

23
F-15C 80-0003 of the 525th TFS(P)/36th TFW, Incirlik AB, Turkey, February 1991

Maj Randy May downed a Mi-24 on 7 February 1991 in this Block 27 F-15C, his kill being one of two *Desert Storm* successes for the Eagle that are surrounded in contention to this day. Firing an AIM-7 into an undercast, the kill was neither confirmed visually, or via intelligence sources on the ground. May was later involved in the tragic friendly fire Blackhawk incident in 1994. Delivered new to the 53rd TFS/36th TFW in August 1981, 80-0003 has served with the 33rd FW since leaving USAFE in April 1994.

24
F-15C 84-0014 of the 53rd TFS/14th AD(P), Prince Sultan AB, Saudi Arabia, March 1991

On 20 March 1991, 84-0014 was used by Capt John Doneski to claim one of the final kills of *Desert Storm* when he downed a single Su-22 'Fitter' with an AIM-7 Sparrow. Doneski currently continues to fly the F-15C on Active Duty, while his jet serves with the 493rd FS at Lakenheath.

Scrap View Commentaries

Notes

Eagle units have traditionally applied unit-specific markings to the inboard sides of the vertical stabilisers. Here is a small selection showing the different styles applied over the years. F-15Cs repainted after *Desert Storm* boasted the 'Mod Eagle' camouflage scheme (FS36251 and FS36176). Originally, all F-15C/Ds were delivered by McDonnell Douglas in FS36320 and FS36375, but they were repainted to 'Mod Eagle' specification as they went through the paint barn on base whilst undergoing routine maintenance.

1

33rd TFW jets used a black band with a cut-out of an Eagle's head overlaid directly onto the existing two-tone grey camouflage until the introduction of 'Mod Eagle'.

2

Bitburg airframes used the black silhouette of an Eagle in flight. This was a more discrete form of artwork than ever seen at Eglin. Again, 'Mod Eagle' resulted in the design changing.

3

With the introduction of the 'Mod Eagle' scheme, the stylised Eagle head was reduced in size and changed slightly to display more feather detail.

4

36th FW F-15C/Ds also changed their Eagle silhouette with the introduction of the low conspicuity camouflage pattern. The silhouette's shape remained unaltered, but was applied in dark grey paint instead.

5

The Eagles of the 493rd FS/48th FW at RAF Lakenheath have never been seen with artwork on their inner fins. The fin flash is gold/yellow, with a black inner band.

6

Similarly, Soesterberg's Eagles displayed only a coloured fin flash. The flash was positioned lower down on the stabiliser in comparison with F-15s from other units, and was (Dutch) orange, with a green trim. The 32nd TFS applied a caricatured Wolfhound on the name plates of its jets, while all other F-15 operators used a feathered Eagle head.

INDEX

References to illustrations are shown in **bold**.Colour plate illustrations are prefixed 'cp.', with page and caption locators in brackets.

Essential Audition So...

male Vocalists pop ballads

IMP

International
MUSIC
Publications

Series Editor: Chris Harvey

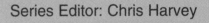

Editorial, Production and Recording: Artemis Music Limited

Design and Production: Space DPS Limited

Published 2002

Ain't No Sunshine

Words and Music by Bill Withers

Bright Eyes

Words and music by Mike Batt

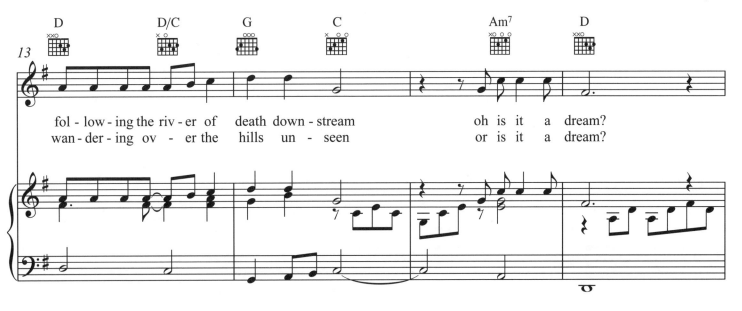

fol - low - ing the riv - er of death down - stream   oh is it a dream?
wan - der - ing ov - er the hills un - seen   or is it a dream?

There's a fog a - long the hor - i - zon   a
There's a high wind in the trees   a

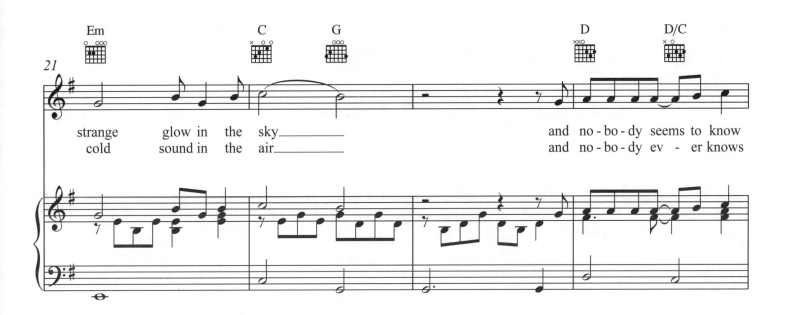

strange glow in the sky   and no - bo - dy seems to know
cold sound in the air   and no - bo - dy ev - er knows

where you go — and what does it mean.
when you go — and where do you start.

Oh oh is it a dream?
Oh oh in - to the dark. ⎱
⎰
Bright eyes—

— burn - ing— like— fire,— bright eyes—

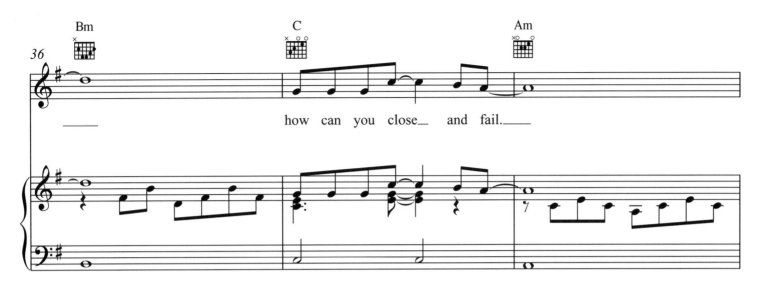

how can you close__ and fail.__

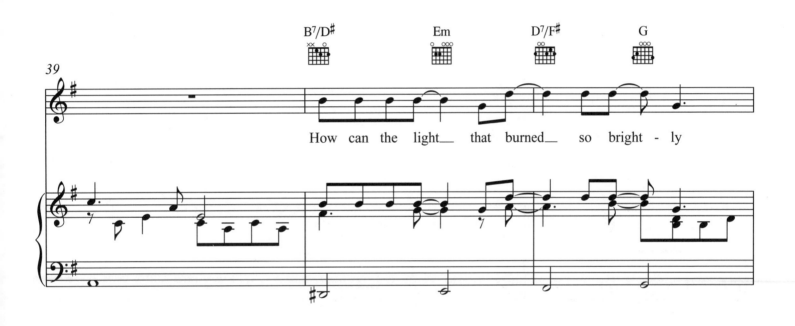

How can the light__ that burned__ so bright - ly

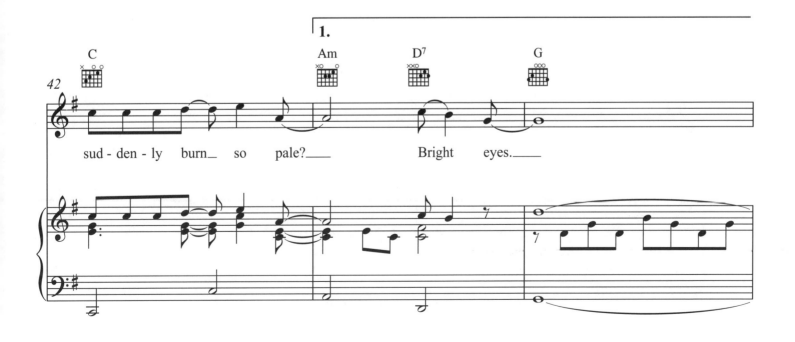

sud - den - ly burn__ so pale?__ Bright eyes.__

Bright eyes,____ Bright eyes.____

Don't Let The Sun
Go Down On Me

Words by Bernie Taupin
Music by Elton John

Backing

Can't Take My Eyes Off You

Words and Music by Bob Crewe and Bob Gaudio

Backing

Careless Whisper

Words and music by George Michael and Andrew Ridgeley

Slow Ballad

1. I feel so——— un - sure——— as I
2. Time can nev - er mend the
3. (To) - night the music seems so loud, I wish that we could lose this crowd, the

way I dance— with you, oh.—

way I dance— with you.—

Repeat ad lib. to fade

Backing

Eternity

Words and Music by Robert Williams and Guy Chambers

Hero

Words and Music by Enrique Iglesias,
Paul Barry and Mark Taylor

Moderately

Spoken: Let me be your hero.

Would you dance   if I asked you to dance?_

—   Would you run   and nev - er look_

Flying Without Wings

Words and Music by Steve Mac and Wayne Hector

How Wonderful You Are

Words and Music by Gordon Haskell

struggled with the art of conversation,—— and there'll be

those—— for whom this song—— has no appeal. But I know it—— works for me, and I'm

sure you will agree,—— that it illustrates exactly how I feel.

Things can—— happen fast, some things are built to last. I've seen it all—— go down in—— Harry's

Right Here Waiting

Words and Music by Richard Marx

Moderately

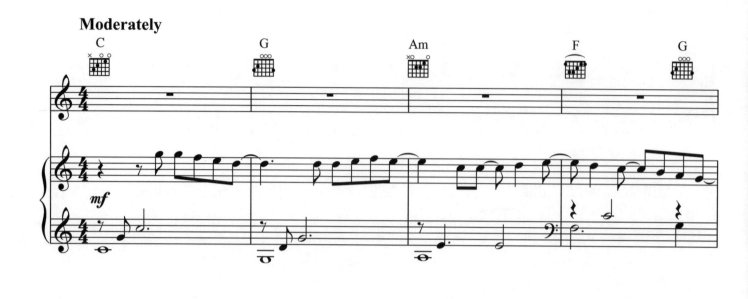

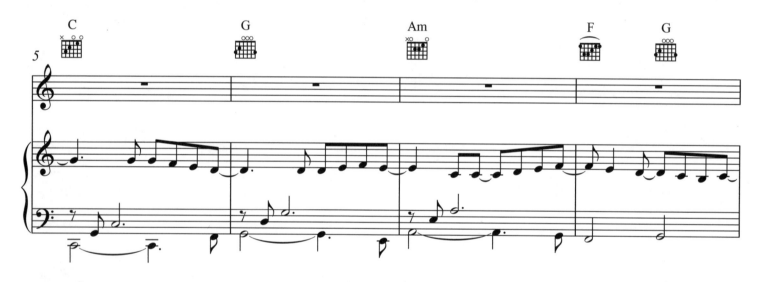

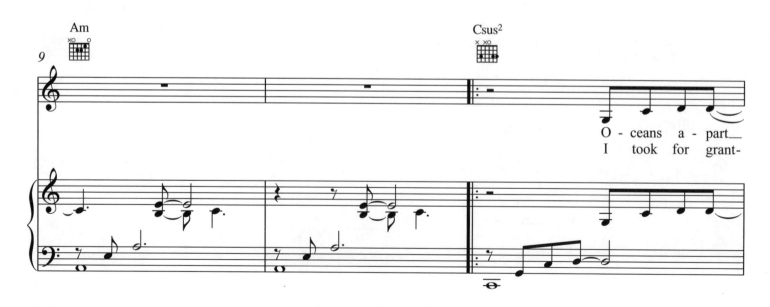

O - ceans a - part___
I took for grant-

 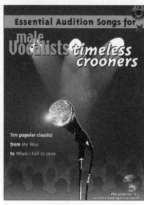  

ESSENTIAL AUDITION SONGS FOR FEMALE VOCALISTS

Broadway
7171A   Book and CD   ISBN: 1859098010

Anything Goes - As Long As He Needs Me - Being Alive - But Not For Me - Fifty Percent - Johnny One Note - Nothing - People - Take Me Or Leave Me - There Won't Be Trumpets

Jazz Standards
7021A   Book and CD   ISBN: 1859097529

Cry Me A River - Desafinado- Ev'ry Time We Say Goodbye - Fever - It's Only A Paper Moon - Mad About The Boy - My Baby Just Cares For Me - Stormy Weather (Keeps Rainin' All The Time) - Summertime - They Can't Take That Away From Me

Pop Ballads
6939A   Book and CD   ISBN: 185909712X

Anything For You - Do You Know Where You're Going To - I Will Always Love You - Killing Me Softly With His - My Heart Will Go On - Over The Rainbow - Promise Me - The Greatest Love Of All- The Way We Were- Walk On By

Pop Divas
7769A   Book and CD   ISBN: 1859099874

Beautiful Stranger - Believe - Genie In A Bottle - I Don't Want To Wait - I Try - Pure Shores - The Greatest Love Of All- Un-Break My Heart - Waiting For Tonight - Without You

ESSENTIAL AUDITION SONGS FOR MALE VOCALISTS

Broadway
9185A   Book and CD   ISBN: 1843280124

Don't Get Around Much Anymore - From Sophisticated Ladies - Get Me To The Church On Time From My Fair Lady - If I Were A Rich Man From Fiddler On The Roof - It Don't Mean A Thing (If It Ain't Got That Swing) From Sophisticated Ladies - It's All Right With Me From Can-Can - On The Street Where You Live From My Fair Lady - Thank Heaven For Little Girls From Gigi - The Lady Is A Tramp From Babes In Arms - Wandrin' Star From Paint Your Wagon - With A Little Bit Of Luck From My Fair Lady

Crooners
9495A   Book and CD   ISBN: 1843280922

Can't Take My Eyes Off You - I Left My Heart In San Francisco - Mack The Knife - My Way - Swingin' On A Star - The Way We Were - Theme From 'New York, New York' - (What A) Wonderful World - When I Fall In Love - Volare

ESSENTIAL AUDITION SONGS FOR FEMALE & MALE VOCALISTS

Duets
7432A   Book and CD   ISBN: 1859099009

Barcelona - Don't Go Breaking My Heart - Endless Love - I Got You Babe - I Knew You Were Waiting (For Me) - (I've Had) The Time Of My Life - It Takes Two - Kids - Nothing's Gonna Stop Us Now - Summer Nights

Essential Audition Songs For Wannabe Pop Stars
9735A   Book and CD   ISBN: 1843282453

Angels - Anything Is Possible - Back For Good - Ev'ry Time We Say Goodbye - Flying Without Wings - Genie In A Bottle - Get Happy - Reach - Up On The Roof - Whole Again

Essential Audition Songs For Kids
7341A   Book and CD   ISBN: 1859098673

Bugsy Malone - Consider Yourself Love's Got A Hold On My Heart Maybe This Time - My Favourite Things - My Name Is Tallulah The Rainbow - We're In The Money Wouldn't It Be Loverly - You're Fully Dressed Without A Smile